2

Vocabulary for the Gifted Student

Written by **Kathy Furgang**

Illustrations by **Valentina Belloni**

FlashKids
New York

FLASH KIDS and the distinctive Flash Kids logo are registered trademarks of
Barnes & Noble, Inc.

Published by Sterling Publishing Co., Inc.
387 Park Avenue South, New York, NY 10016
Text and illustrations © 2011 by Flash Kids
Distributed in Canada by Sterling Publishing
c/o Canadian Manda Group, 165 Dufferin Street
Toronto, Ontario, Canada M6K 3H6
Distributed in the United Kingdom by GMC Distribution Services
Castle Place, 166 High Street, Lewes, East Sussex, England BN7 1XU
Distributed in Australia by Capricorn Link (Australia) Pty. Ltd.
P.O. Box 704, Windsor, NSW 2756, Australia

Sterling ISBN 978-1-4114-2768-6

Manufactured in Canada

Lot #:
2   4   6   8   10   9   7   5   3   1
03/11

For information about custom editions, special sales, premium and
corporate purchases, please contact Sterling Special Sales
Department at 800-805-5489 or specialsales@sterlingpublishing.com.

Cover image © by Glow Images/Getty Images
Cover design and production by Mada Design, Inc.

Dear Parents,

If your child is ready for a challenge, *Vocabulary for the Gifted Student* is a perfect opportunity to introduce skills and concepts that will be useful in the years to come.

The enriching vocabulary in this book focuses on diverse subjects such as technology, dictionary skills, geography, American history, meteorology, art, and grammar. Children will be introduced to both second-grade and above-level words through reading passages, as well as engaging thinking, writing, and drawing activities. Concepts such as prefixes, suffixes, homophones, compound words, synonyms, antonyms, and multiple meaning words are introduced and reinforced.

Reading passages have a reading level of one- to one-and-a-half grade levels above his or her current grade. Lexile levels for the above-level second grade student are at approximately 500 to 750.

As your child becomes more familiar with the vocabulary, he or she will move from word searches and crossword puzzles to fill in the blanks, hidden pictures, and writing activities such as poetry. Every section of new vocabulary is revisited in a two-page review called "Let's Go Over That Again."

Encourage your child to work independently to answer questions about the vocabulary being introduced, offering assistance when needed. More importantly, provide opportunities for your child to use the new words in conversation. Practice makes perfect!

Word Search

There are eight words hidden in the puzzle. Use the definitions below to help you find them. Then write the words next to their meanings.

```
J  K  I  O  M  R  W  X  J  A
H  M  E  A  S  U  R  E  P  O
F  Q  K  I  I  O  Z  L  L  X
C  W  S  V  B  N  T  T  G  N
A  C  B  D  E  S  T  R  O  Y
G  T  C  E  S  R  J  D  Q  S
R  I  R  N  S  B  R  H  U  T
E  R  M  E  M  N  T  Y  X  E
E  E  V  M  B  F  A  D  R  M
I  O  P  Y  F  L  A  T  W  A
C  V  B  N  K  L  Q  F  G  E
E  I  U  O  W  O  R  R  A  N
```

1. to think the same way as someone else _____

2. to ruin _____

3. the opposite of friend _____

4. smooth and even _____

5. to tell how far or how heavy _____

6. not wide _____

7. plant part that holds up a flower _____

8. a rubber wheel _____

Find the Opposite Word

Read each question. To find the answer, fill in the blank with the opposite of the underlined word.

1. Do you <u>disagree</u> with me?

No, I _____ with you!

2. Will you <u>build</u> the sandcastle?

No, I will _____ the sandcastle!

3. Is the road <u>hilly</u>?

No, the road is _____.

4. Is he your <u>friend</u>?

No, he is my _____!

5. Is the hallway <u>wide</u>?

No, the hallway is _____!

Fill in the Blanks

Fill in the blanks in the story. Use the words in the box.

agree   destroy   enemy   flat

measure   narrow   stem   tire

Grandma just loves her rose bush. She talks about it all the time. But last week, Mom ran over it with her car! She crashed into the biggest _____ on the plant. It was _____ on the ground in two seconds. I'm sure there are still thorns stuck in the rubber of the _____ !

Grandma came out of the house with her hands in the air.

"Oh no!" she cried. "Why did you _____ my beautiful rose bush?"

"That driveway is my worst _____ !" said Mom

Maybe we should _____ the driveway with a ruler. I think it's a little bit too _____ for our giant car. Even so, we can all _____ that it wasn't the driveway's fault. Mom just needs to drive more carefully!

Make Your Own Story

Write your own story below. Use as many of the
words as possible from the box below.

agree	destroy	enemy	flat
measure	narrow	stem	tire

_____

_____

_____

_____

_____

_____

_____

_____

Crossword Time!

Use the clues below to solve the crossword puzzle.
Use the words from the word box.

agree   destroy   enemy   flat

measure   narrow   stem   tire

Across
1. not round
3. to tell how long
6. to say yes
7. not a friend

Down
2. plant part
4. to ruin
5. rubber wheel
6. not wide

Measure Up!

There are many ways to measure. Draw or write a list of ways you can measure. The first one is done for you.

1. A ruler measures how _____long_____ something is.

2. A scale measures how _____ something is.

3. A thermometer measures how _____ something is.

4. A cup measures how _____ you have of something.

5. List things that you can measure!

_____

_____

_____

Let's Go Over That Again

Review. Fill in each blank with a word from the box.
Then write your own sentence using the word.

agree   destroy   enemy   flat

1. Someone who is not a friend is an _____.

_____

2. The part of a car or bike that is attached to the wheel is the _____.

_____

3. When you think the same as a person, you _____ with him.

_____

4. One part of a plant is called the _____.

_____

measure   narrow   stem   tire

5. To tell how long or how hot something is, you must _____.

_____

6. Something that is not wide is called _____.

_____

7. When something is smooth and even, it is _____.

_____

8. When you ruin something, you _____ it.

_____

Leah the Tightrope Walker

Read the story. Then answer the questions below.

Leah's family has been in the circus business for almost a century. She lives with clowns, acrobats, and animal tamers. There is always something fun happening. For her, life is a carnival.

Leah wants to work in the circus some day, too. She dreams of walking the tightrope. When she turned eight, her cousin began giving her lessons.

Now it is time for Leah to show what she has been learning for the past few months. Today will be her first attempt at doing the tightrope walk during a circus performance.

She knows she has to fight off her fears. She will be strong and not let this rattle her nerves.

Up she climbs to the circus big top. She looks out over the crowd.

"It's now or never," she says to herself. She focuses her mind and performs her routine perfectly.

1. What does the word **attempt** mean in the passage?

   a. hurt   **b.** try   **c.** scare

2. What is another way to say "rattle her nerves"?

   a. make her scared   **b.** make her happy   **c.** make her confused

3. Why is Leah's life like a carnival?

   a. It is boring.   **b.** It is sad.   **c.** It is like a celebration.

4. What does the word **century** mean?

   a. 100 years   **b.** 50 years   **c.** 10 years

Just a Figure of Speech

Read the story on page 12 again. Make a drawing to illustrate the phrase "fight off her fears" or "rattle her nerves." Then describe your drawing.

Word Search

There are nine words hidden in the puzzle. Use the definitions below to help you find them. Then write the words next to their meanings.

```
G  R  E  A  G  M  X  Y  L  W
C  E  N  T  U  R  Y  J  E  T
A  V  S  O  I  A  K  C  B  M
R  F  W  C  Y  T  P  O  D  E
N  O  O  A  T  T  E  M  P  T
I  T  E  S  R  L  R  T  D  O
V  H  T  H  E  E  Z  C  C  S
A  G  E  B  R  T  S  E  Y  S
L  I  T  O  P  W  Z  E  U  D
U  F  S  T  R  O  N  G  E  H
M  J  D  U  Y  M  C  H  O  P
```

1. to try _____

2. fair or circus _____

3. money _____

4. one hundred years _____

5. to cut _____

6. battle or argument _____

7. to shake _____

8. powerful _____

9. to throw lightly _____

Picture Search

Look for pictures that show each of the words in the box below.
Circle each picture.

carnival   cash   chop

rattle   strong   toss

Fill in the Blanks

Fill in the blanks in the story. Use the words in the box.

attempt   century   fight

strong   toss

Did you know that chimpanzees _____ with one another? A _____ ago people did not know much about these animals. But scientists have tried to learn more. Jane Goodall observed chimpanzees in Africa for many years. She noticed that they sometimes fought each other. She even saw that groups of chimps would go to war with each other!

These animals can be _____. They might _____ things at each other. They might _____ to hurt each other. But for the most part, chimpanzees are peaceful animals! They are afraid of people. They live in groups and care for each other. They are not that different from you and me!

Crossword Time!

Use the clues below to solve the crossword puzzle.
Use the words from the word box.

attempt   carnival   cash   chop

rattle   strong   toss   century   flight

Across
1. a fair
2. to shake
3. to try
6. to cut

Down
1. 100 years
4. bold
5. to throw lightly
7. money
8. to battle

Say It a Different Way

Read each question. To find the answer, fill in the blank
with a word that means the same as the underlined word.

attempt   carnival   cash   chop

rattle   strong   toss

1. Do you have any <u>money</u>?

Yes, I have _____ in my pocket.

2. Will you <u>cut</u> the carrots for the stew?

Yes, I will _____ the vegetables.

3. Could you <u>shake</u> your keys?

Yes, I will _____ the keys.

4. Are you going to the <u>fair</u>?

Yes, I am going to the _____.

5. Will you <u>throw</u> me that pillow?

Yes, I will _____ you the pillow.

6. Will you <u>try</u> to win the game?

Yes, I will _____ to win the game.

7. Will the storm be <u>powerful</u>?

Yes, the storm will be _____.

Thinking About Time

Think of something that was invented in the last century. Draw it and write about how it changed the way we live in this century.

Let's Go Over That Again

Review. Fill in each blank with a word from the box.
Then write your own sentence using the word.

attempt   carnival   cash   century

1. A person who is powerful is _____.

_____

2. To throw something lightly is to _____ it.

_____

3. A battle is a kind of a _____.

_____

4. When you try something, you make an _____ at it.

_____

5. A _____ is like a fair or a circus.

_____

chop   fight   rattle   strong   toss

6. To shake something is to _____ it.

_____

7. A one hundred year period is called a _____.

_____

8. Another word for money is _____.

_____

9. When you cut something, you _____ it.

_____

Winter Break Is Over

Read the story. Then answer the questions below.

Today was the first day back from winter break. I was looking forward to getting back to school. I spent a lot of time over the break taking care of my little brother. I must have changed about a dozen diapers!

I had a very good, or positive, feeling when I went to school this morning. But things changed quickly. Almost the minute we got off the bus we were greeted with a surprise math quiz! My positive mood quickly turned negative.

The first few questions were easy, but then things became harder. We had to put negative numbers on a number line. I was very unsure about the answers.

But later in the day we got our grades. I got everything right! My negative mood turned positive once again.

1. What does the word **positive** mean in the second paragraph?
   a. feeling   **b.** good   **c.** bad

2. What does the word **negative** mean in the second paragraph?
   a. mood   **b.** good   **c.** bad

3. What does the word **negative** mean in the third paragraph?
   a. less than zero   **b.** more than zero   **c.** unsure

4. What is the relation between the words **positive** and **negative** in the last paragraph?
   a. They are synonyms.   **b.** They are antonyms.
   c. They have to do with numbers.

Find Them All!

There are seven words hidden in the puzzle. Use the definitions below to help you find them. Then write the words next to their meanings.

```
K  G  S  O  U  U  T  W  H  E
B  O  U  G  H  T  B  I  J  V
I  W  O  W  F  A  I  L  T  I
C  O  M  I  A  G  B  D  Z  T
N  T  A  Q  U  U  K  G  N  A
V  E  F  N  B  C  E  F  N  G
E  V  E  R  Y  W  H  E  R  E
O  U  M  G  X  O  R  K  T  N
E  U  N  I  T  N  O  C  O  Y
R  S  B  V  K  L  D  Y  D  E
```

1. purchased _____

2. to go on _____

3. all over the place _____

4. the opposite of pass _____

5. well-known around the world _____

6. the opposite of positive _____

7. not able to control _____

Fill In the Blanks

Practice present and past tenses. Fill in the correct words in the blanks below. The first one is done for you.

Present Tense	Past Tense
1. continue	continued
2. buy	_____
3. _____	sold
4. _____	failed
5. stop	_____
6. _____	succeeded
7. teach	_____

Crossword Time!

Solve the crossword puzzle below by finding the **opposite** word from the clue.

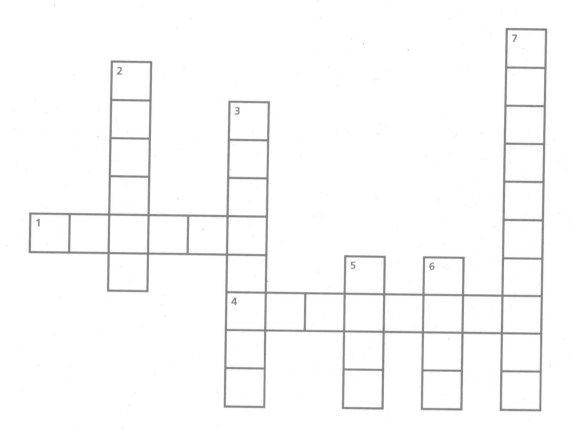

Across
1. sold
4. positive

Down
2. unknown
3. stop
5. succeed
6. calm
7. nowhere

The Wild, Wild West

Read the passage. Then answer the questions below.

The time in the 1800s when American settlers moved across the plains to the western part of the United States is often called the Wild West. How did it get such a name? The word wild means out of control. And that's just what the western frontier was. There were few laws in place. There were also few police forces or jails to put criminals in.

The land in the West could also be rough. People had to struggle to survive. People did not want to take such a dangerous journey and fail. They would continue on their journey the best they could.

The Wild West became famous for lawlessness. It was a dangerous place to settle a family. But over time, the American West became settled. Now it is one of the most scenic and beautiful places in our country.

1. What does the word **wild** mean?

_____

2. What does the word **continue** mean?

_____

3. What does the word **fail** mean?

_____

4. Look at the word **lawlessness**. What is the root word? _____

What are two suffixes in the word?

_____   _____

5. What does the word **settled** mean?

_____

Make Your Own Word Search!

Write the five words below in the word search by putting each letter in a box. You can write them in any direction. Then fill in the extra boxes with other letters that do not spell any words. Lastly, write a sentence clue for each word below. Give your puzzle to a friend to solve.

bought   continue   everywhere

famous   negative

1. _____

2. _____

3. _____

4. _____

5. _____

Let's Go Over That Again

Review. Circle the opposite of each word.
Then write a sentence that uses both words.

1. fail   succeed   try

_____

2. famous   popular   unknown

_____

3. bought   sold   buy

_____

4. continue   go   stop

_____

5. negative   bad   positive

_____

6. everywhere   nowhere   somewhere

_____

7. wild   silly   calm

_____

Review. Choose the meaning of the underlined word.

1. Layla <u>bought</u> three apples today.
   a. sold
   b. paid money for
   c. made

2. Cooper does not want to <u>fail</u> the test.
   a. take
   b. correct
   c. not pass

3. Carrie had a <u>negative</u> feeling about the party.
   a. good
   b. bad
   c. fun

4. Leo saw a <u>famous</u> person on the street today.
   a. lost
   b. well-known
   c. funny

5. The woods are filled with <u>wild</u> animals.
   a. well-behaved
   b. large
   c. out of control

Hidden Pictures

Look for pictures that show each of the words in the box below.
Circle each picture.

bicycle   blueberry   broom   doorway
elevator   fireworks   litter   stone

Word Search

There are eight words hidden in the puzzle. Use the definitions below to help you find them. Then write the words next to their meanings.

```
H  S  K  R  O  W  E  R  I  F
Y  R  O  S  T  O  N  E  G  X
R  W  T  R  L  G  C  N  E  I
R  B  K  L  E  O  M  T  F  Y
E  L  E  V  A  T  O  R  W  I
B  I  V  K  L  A  O  T  T  R
E  T  P  D  O  O  R  W  A  Y
U  T  J  Y  R  T  B  U  E  L
L  E  B  I  C  Y  C  L  E  P
B  R  E  R  H  B  S  E  U  O
```

1. you ride it on two wheels _____

2. a blue fruit _____

3. a tool to clean the floor _____

4. found between rooms _____

5. carries people up and down floors _____

6. explosions of light in the sky _____

7. garbage pollution _____

8. rock _____

Clara's Saturday Morning

Read the story. Underline each word in the
word box as you read it in the story.

bicycle   blueberry   broom   doorway
elevator   fireworks   litter   stone

Clara spent most of the morning picking blueberries from the woods outside her farmhouse. She piled the berries into a small pail and put them on the back of her bicycle.

But this morning, Clara was up for a new kind of adventure. She rode into town to see the work crews setting up for tonight's fireworks display. The crews left litter on the ground with each fireworks package they opened. *Those boys can use a good broom*, Clara thought to herself.

Then Clara pushed her bike across the grass to Jesse's Coffee Shop. She noticed the carved stone above the doorway of the shop. She and her dad made that for Aunt Jesse when she opened her shop last year. It said "All Are Welcome."

Jesse saw Clara coming.

"A pail of blueberries!" said Aunt Jesse. "Can I buy those from you? I am all out of blueberry muffins for the shop."

"Sure, Aunt Jesse," said Clara. "I just picked them this morning!"

Continue the Story...

Continue the story from page 32.
Use all eight words from the word box.

bicycle   blueberry   broom   doorway
elevator   fireworks   litter   stone

_____

_____

_____

_____

_____

_____

_____

_____

Make Compound Words

Draw a line from each word on the left to a word
on the right that makes a compound word.

blue   works

door   berry

fire   way

Write the compound words you found.

1. _____

2. _____

3. _____

Use each compound word above in a sentence.

4. _____

5. _____

6. _____

Crossword Time!

Use the clues below to solve the crossword puzzle.
Use the words from the word box.

broom   doorway   elevator   bicycle

stone   fireworks   blueberry   litter

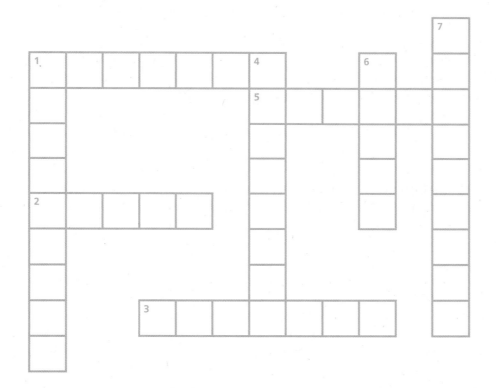

Across

1. something you ride on

2. something you use to clean floors

3. something you walk through

5. garbage left on the ground

Down

1. a fruit

4. something used instead of stairs

6. a rock

7. explosions of light in the sky

Let's Go Over That Again

Review. Answer each question below.

1. Which of these is a fruit?
   a. carrot
   b. blueberry
   c. corn

2. Which of these can be used to clean a kitchen floor?
   a. broom
   b. rake
   c. shovel

3. Which of these must you walk through to get into a house?
   a. couch
   b. refrigerator
   c. doorway

4. Which of these is left behind when people are not careful?
   a. litter
   b. sunshine
   c. clouds

5. Which of these can be driven by a child?
   a. car
   b. airplane
   c. bicycle

6. Which of these can be used instead of stairs?
   a. elevator
   b. motorcycle
   c. stove

7. Which of these is the easiest to lift?
   a. boulder
   b. stone
   c. tree

8. Which of these are used at large celebrations?
   a. fireworks
   b. puzzles
   c. rafts

Word Search

There are six words hidden in the puzzle. Use the definitions below to help you find them. Then write the words next to their meanings.

```
R  D  O  K  A  I  Y  L  U  T  S  H
O  B  U  W  L  G  B  H  P  O  E  U
E  A  F  O  L  H  S  I  B  N  T  K
G  S  C  P  L  E  N  T  I  F  U  L
W  I  Y  L  D  N  M  X  Y  K  D  C
D  C  R  E  D  K  P  H  B  V  I  H
H  P  K  D  M  N  E  D  S  W  I  S
O  U  T  S  T  A  N  D  I  N  G  I
R  O  K  D  V  S  P  E  C  I  A  L
T  H  C  W  M  Q  O  J  O  C  P  O
Y  W  O  Q  B  M  U  Y  E  I  T  O
L  U  F  E  C  R  O  F  H  F  B  F
```

1. simple _____

2. silly _____

3. using force _____

4. amazing _____

5. having many _____

6. better or greater _____

Draw Mr. Bubbles

Mr. Bubbles is an outstanding baker. Draw him in his kitchen.
Show that you know what the word "outstanding" means.
Write a sentence to describe your picture.

_____

_____

Fun with Adjectives

The words in the box below are all adjectives. They describe a noun. Write each adjective with a noun to describe it. Then draw a humorous picture of each adjective and noun. The first one has been done for you.

1. foolish  dog

2. forceful _____

3. outstanding _____

4. plentiful _____

5. special _____

Crossword Time!

Use the clues below to solve the crossword puzzle.
Use the words from the word box.

basic foolish forceful

outstanding plentiful special

Across

1. not plain
5. not weak
6. not empty

Down

2. not ordinary
3. not complex
4. not smart

Test Your Dictionary Skills

Put the dictionary entries in alphabetical order on the lines below.
Write a new sentence for each word.

force•ful |'fôrsfŭl|
adjective
strong and powerful: *She can be a forceful person.*

plen•ti•ful |'plentĭfŭl|
adjective
in great quantities; a lot: *The good weather was plentiful this summer.*

ba•sic |'bāsik|
adjective
simplest, or lowest level: *We want only basic answers to our questions.*

_____

_____

_____

_____

_____

_____

_____

_____

Explain the Saying

There is a saying that goes, "There are no foolish questions, only foolish silence." What do you think the saying means? Explain the saying below. Give an example.

_____

_____

_____

_____

_____

_____

_____

The Honey Harvest

Read the story. Then answer the questions below.

Bob's bees had a great season. They buzzed along all spring and summer and made a plentiful harvest of honey for the hive. Bob regularly emptied the extra honey from the hive and bottled it up. He brought it to market and made money for his family.

But a few of the bees in the hive thought they could live alone and make their own honey just for themselves. Buzz and Frankie thought they could do it. They did not want to make honey for Bob and his family. They thought they were special. They wanted to make honey for themselves.

Their plan failed miserably. It is a foolish bee that thinks that he can live alone. Bees are very social creatures, and they work in groups to make the honey for the hive. It provides the hive's babies with their basic food needs.

1. Which word from the passage means **out of the ordinary**?
   a. special   **b.** miserably   **c.** social

2. Which word from the passage means **simple**?
   a. foolish   **b.** regularly   **c.** basic

3. Which word from the passage means **a lot**?
   a. special   **b.** plentiful   **c.** alone

4. There are four adjectives in the last paragraph. Write them here.

_____   _____

_____   _____

Write a Poem

Think about the word "special." Choose a person or thing that is special in your life. Write a poem about it.
Your poem should tell why that person or thing is special.

_____

_____

_____

_____

_____

_____

_____

Let's Go Over That Again

Review. Answer the questions below.

1. A forceful person is _____.
   a. strong
   b. weak
   c. unhappy

2. An outstanding performance is an _____ one.
   a. elegant
   b. excellent
   c. important

3. A plentiful penny collection is a _____ one.
   a. clean
   b. large
   c. new

4. A basic need is a _____ one.
   a. simple
   b. strong
   c. silly

5. A special day is one that is _____.
   a. not usual
   b. ordinary
   c. long

6. A foolish person is one who does not have good _____.
   a. friends
   b. manners
   c. sense

Fill in the Blanks

Read the paragraph below. Fill in the blanks with the words from the word box.

basic   foolish   forceful

outstanding   plentiful   special

We are looking forward to acting in Jane's new play. It is a _____ chance to show how well we can perform. Last year's show was so _____ that the audience stood and cheered for us! It would be _____ to pass by this great opportunity.

The play is about three friends with _____ personalities. One character is really funny. He has a_____ collection of baseball cards. The funny part is that he won't show it to anyone! That is the _____ idea of the play. I can't wait to read the whole thing.

Homophones!

Homophones are words that sound alike, but have different meanings and different spellings. Underline the homophone pairs in each sentence. Then check whether they are used correctly or incorrectly.

1. I know horses don't usually talk, but this one sounded hoarse!

   ❑ Correct   ❑ Incorrect

2. The sail for the boat is on sale at the store.

   ❑ Correct   ❑ Incorrect

3. I plug in the chord for my electric guitar so that I can play a musical cord.

   ❑ Correct   ❑ Incorrect

4. Every knight Billy dresses up like a night.

   ❑ Correct   ❑ Incorrect

5. I can smell the rows of flowers, even the rose.

   ❑ Correct   ❑ Incorrect

6. Does the hair have white hare or gray hare?

   ❑ Correct   ❑ Incorrect

Drawing Homophones

Draw a picture to illustrate each sentence.

1. Draw a doe rolling dough.

2. Draw an animal with a tail who is reading a tale.

3. Draw a male opening some mail.

4. Draw a flower next to a bag of flour.

Word Search

There are eight words hidden in the puzzle. Use the definitions below to help you find them. Then write the words next to their meanings.

```
L  I  A  M  G  R  O  N
W  D  M  A  L  E  T  E
C  K  L  H  D  S  U  K
E  H  G  H  O  R  B  N
D  O  U  G  H  A  S  I
O  R  C  K  L  O  I  G
E  S  G  A  I  H  Y  H
S  E  E  N  I  G  H  T
```

1. flour mixture used to make bread _____

2. a female deer _____

3. letters that go through the post office _____

4. not a female _____

5. four-legged riding animal _____

6. a rough-sounding voice _____

7. soldier from the Middle Ages _____

8. the opposite of day _____

Crossword Puzzle!

Write the homophone for each word in the crossword puzzle.

Across
1. flour
3. tow
5. sea

Down
1. fare
2. weight
4. rows

Fill in the Blanks

Fill in the blank in each sentence with the correct homophone.

1. We can _____ until dessert to eat the cake.

weight   wait

2. I think it will rain all _____ long.

night   knight

3. Mom gave me a _____ after the show.

rows   rose

4. I like to brush the _____ in the barn.

hoarse   horse

5. Don't forget to unplug the lamp _____.

cord   chord

6. I bought five apples on _____ at the store.

sail   sale

7. You can use _____ to make the bread.

flour   flower

Fix the Homophones

Underline the errors with homophones in the paragraph below.
Rewrite the paragraph correctly in the space below.

When I road my hoarse to the fare, I was excited to see my friends. I could see that Jessica got her hare cut short. She looked grate! She gave me a rows. She got it on sail at the flour stand near the front entrance of the fair. We went to get a snack. My favorite thing is the fried doe. I could eat a hole plate of it!

_____

_____

_____

_____

_____

_____

_____

Find More Homophones!

There are eight words hidden in the puzzle. Use the definitions below to help you find them. Then write the words next to their meanings.

```
R   O   R   I   A   F   U   W
D   G   O   G   A   R   F   E
E   R   A   D   L   P   A   W
L   E   D   U   O   E   R   S
O   A   W   H   O   L   E   X
H   T   O   P   A   G   N   J
S   C   D   G   R   A   T   E
B   R   O   D   E   I   E   W
```

1. wonderful _____

2. to shred _____

3. following the rules _____

4. money needed to do something _____

5. the past tense of ride _____

6. a street _____

7. all of it _____

8. an opening _____

Write a Sentence of Homophones

Write a sentence to describe each picture.
Use a homophone pair in each sentence.

1.

_____

_____

_____

2.

_____

_____

_____

3.

_____

_____

_____

4.

_____

_____

_____

Let's Go Over That Again

Review. Choose the correct homophone to complete each sentence.

1. The word **grate** means
   a. to shred something
   b. wonderful

2. The word **hoarse** means
   a. an animal
   b. rough sounding

3. The word **fare** means
   a. money needed to do something
   b. a carnival or amusement

4. The word **chord** means
   a. a wire that plugs into the wall
   b. a combination of musical notes

5. The word **rode** means
   a. the past tense of ride
   b. a wide path leading from one place to another

6. The word **whole** means
   a. the entire amount
   b. a hollow place for something to fit inside

7. The word **night** means
   a. the opposite of day
   b. a person from the Middle Ages who wore protective armor

8. The word **flour** means
   a. a part of a plant
   b. a powder made from grinding grain

9. The word **sail** means
   a. able to be sold
   b. a material used on a boat to catch the wind

10. The word **hare** means
   a. a long-eared mammal
   b. threadlike fibers that grow on humans and other mammals

Nina and the Squirrels

Read the story. Then answer the questions below.

The autumn leaves just began falling and the weather had not yet become bitter cold. It was Nina's favorite time of year. She felt an instant happiness when she went outside on fall mornings. She felt alive and ready to tackle the day.

But today was a little different. She noticed that the squirrels were having trouble gathering food. Everywhere they looked, they came up dry. She felt pity for the animals. But she knew that she should  not interfere with wildlife. You are not supposed to get wildlife used to people. If you do, they will feel less afraid. They may rely on people for food. Nina certainly didn't want another animal to capture the squirrels because they were not on their guard. Animals in the woods were very tricky. They would do anything to con the squirrels and then eat them for lunch! Instead, Nina continued on her way. She knew the squirrels would gather enough food before the weather got too cold. That's their job, after all. They could probably do it much better than Nina could!

1. In which season does the story take place?

_____

2. What does the word **bitter** mean?

_____

3. What does the word **instant** mean in paragraph 1?

_____

4. What does the author mean by the word **pity**?

_____

Word Search

There are eight words hidden in the puzzle. Use the definitions below to help you find them. Then write the words next to their meanings.

```
E   S   N   O   B   T   L   V
R   E   T   T   I   B   H   C
U   J   N   Q   U   A   K   O
T   E   A   U   T   U   M   N
P   Y   T   L   J   B   E   O
A   U   S   I   I   P   T   P
C   H   N   W   C   V   C   I
A   X   I   Y   P   N   E   T
S   M   A   G   N   I   F   Y
U   J   L   P   Y   E   O   N
```

1. living _____

2. the season also called fall _____

3. a sharp or sour taste _____

4. to catch _____

5. to trick or swindle _____

6. sudden or on-the-spot _____

7. to make larger _____

8. a shame _____

Which Story Is Correct?

Read the stories. Circle the one that uses the underlined words correctly.
Then draw a picture to illustrate that story.

1. Marge was a private detective. She knew how to spot a <u>con</u> from a mile away. Last <u>autumn</u>, she discovered that Dave was cheating Lou's Grocery out of money. To capture him, she pretended to be a worker. She knew in an <u>instant</u> that he gave her fake money. There wasn't a person <u>alive</u> who would be fooled by his dishonesty! Soon everyone would know about it. The police would <u>capture</u> Dave.

2. Marge was a private <u>con</u>. On a snowy day in <u>autumn</u>, she began a plan to <u>capture</u> a plan. She knew that the criminal would be very <u>alive</u> when he was caught. It would take her weeks to find him. It would be a long <u>instant</u>.

The Story Goes On

Write a simple ending to the story on page 60.
Use the words **magnify**, **bitter**, and **pity** in your story.
Draw a picture that goes with your story.

Crossword Time!

Solve the crossword puzzle by filling in the blanks with the correct vocabulary word in the sentences below.

Across

1. One of the four seasons is _____.

5. The lightning was over in an _____.

6. It's a _____ that she is sick.

Down

2. The lime tastes _____.

3. The lens will _____ the object.

4. The game was a trick, or a _____.

7. It's great to be _____!

8. I will _____ the fish in the net and the let it go.

Put Them in Order

Put the words below in alphabetical order in the middle of the circle.

instant capture pity autumn magnify con alive bitter

_____

_____

_____

_____

_____

_____

_____

_____

Let's Go Over That Again

Review. Answer the questions below.

1. The season when leaves fall from trees is _____.
   a. spring
   b. summer
   c. autumn

2. Something that is living is _____.
   a. alive
   b. rock
   c. nonliving

3. When you make something bigger, you _____ it.
   a. magnify
   b. wake
   c. reduce

4. Another word for a trick is a _____.
   a. treat
   b. con
   c. sickness

5. When something tastes harsh or unpleasant, it may taste
_____.

    a. sweet
    b. pleasant
    c. bitter

6. When you feel badly for someone, you _____ them.
    a. pity
    b. fill
    c. wonder

7. To catch something means to _____ it.
    a. release
    b. capture
    c. sign

8. When it only takes a second to do something, it takes an
_____.

    a. instant
    b. unknown
    c. hour

Prefixes, Prefixes

Circle the words in each row that have
the same prefix as the first word in the row.

1. prefix	preview	popcorn	perfect	prevent
2. disappear	detain	dislike	disagree	deliver
3. midstream	marker	midterm	maple	midline
4. nonsense	nonstop	napkin	narrator	narrow
5. inside	into	indirect	important	inflate

Circle the Base Word

A **base word** is a word without a prefix or suffix attached to it. Look at each word below. Circle the base word. Underline the prefix.

mistake

unsafe

preheat

impossible

discover

inside

export

impolite

Match Them Up!

Draw a line from the prefix in the left column to
the base word in the right column.

1.   re   happy

2.   non   arm

3.   un   side

4.   tele   view

5.   fore   phone

6.   in   sense

Word Search

There are seven words hidden in the puzzle. Use the definitions below to help you find them. Then write the words next to their meanings.

```
P   R   E   S   C   H   O   O   L
E   E   H   K   U   E   N   U   E
V   P   U   N   E   V   E   N   R
I   L   H   T   J   P   E   D   D
L   A   E   Y   D   R   F   O   I
E   Y   D   I   S   M   I   S   S
R   W   C   D   E   M   X   I   R
L   T   N   I   A   P   E   R   Y
```

1. school for the youngest children _____

2. to let go _____

3. to play again _____

4. to take apart _____

5. to live again _____

6. not even _____

7. to paint again _____

Crossword Time!

Use the clues below to solve the crossword puzzle.
Use the words from the word box.

unsafe   relive   unkind   review   disobey

Across

1. not kind

3. to view again

Down

1. not safe

2. to not obey

4. to live again

Prefix Unscramble

Unscramble each word below.

1. thpreea   _____

2. hpapnuy   _____

3. eeonnssn   _____

4. sidybeo   _____

5. runaif   _____

6. doer   _____

7. ttrsimea   _____

8. vcnureo   _____

Sonny's Sunny Morning

Read the story. Then answer the questions below.

Every morning Sonny got up out of bed and previewed the day before her. She made her bed, ate breakfast, and brushed her teeth. Then she walked her dog.

Sonny would be very unhappy if things did not happen in this order every morning. She thought of any change in her plan to be nonsense. Sonny did not have time for nonsense before school.

But this day was already not going as planned. The dog disobeyed her when she called for him. It was impossible to get him out of the house. Then suddenly, Sonny had a bright idea. She ran out the door and twirled around in the sunshine. The dog stared at her for a few moments. That's when he discovered what a beautiful, sunny day it really was. He jumped through the doggie door and leapt into Sonny's arms. Success! Maybe she would make it to school on time today after all.

1. What does the word **previewed** mean in the story?

_____

2. What is the prefix in the word **unhappy**? What does the prefix mean?

_____

3. What is the base of the word **disobeyed**? What does the word mean?

_____

4. What is the opposite of the word **impossible**?

_____

What Do the Prefixes Mean?

Write the meaning of each prefix below.

1.

2.

3.

4.

5.

6.

Let's Go Over That Again

Review. Underline each prefix. Write the meaning of each word.

1. We went to a **preview** of the movie last night.

_____

2. Jan had to **repaint** the garage door.

_____

3. The icing on the cake was **uneven**.

_____

4. We can **replay** your scene from the play.

_____

5. Liam wants to **relive** the funny parts of the play.

_____

6. It is **impossible** to chew and whistle at the same time.

_____

7. You should not **disobey** the teacher!

_____

8. I heard the **telephone** ring a few minutes ago.

_____

9. The book was funny because it was **nonsense**.

_____

10. It would be **impolite** to talk while the teacher is talking.

_____

Geography Compound Words

There are eight words hidden in the puzzle. Use the definitions below to help you find them. Then write the words next to their meanings.

```
A  G  D  T  U  V  W  H  B  W  D  S
R  R  U  Q  V  D  P  D  X  H  G  L
C  A  A  O  P  J  U  E  R  I  M  T
A  S  E  K  A  U  Q  H  T  R  A  E
O  S  T  I  D  E  P  O  O  L  E  Q
P  L  S  F  U  L  O  D  L  P  T  T
L  A  N  D  M  A  S  S  W  O  H  W
H  N  C  B  U  M  U  L  O  O  E  O
J  D  N  R  D  O  T  P  R  L  J  O
M  O  U  N  T  A  I  N  T  O  P  R
E  C  O  U  N  T  R  Y  S  I  D  E
W  E  M  R  O  F  D  N  A  L  Y  S
```

1. land covered in grass _____

2. a small pool of tide water _____

3. a formation of land _____

4. scenic land away from a city _____

5. water moving in a circle _____

6. shaking or quaking of earth _____

7. a mass of land _____

8. top of a mountain _____

Crossword Puzzle!

Use the clues below to solve the crossword puzzle.

Across

1. the top of a mountain

3. a moving, or swirling, body of water

4. a flat, grassy area

Down

2. a natural pool of water left behind by moving tides

5. a natural feature of Earth's land

Beautiful Places, Unhappy Faces

Read the story. Then answer the questions below.

Janie's family moved from the city to the countryside. Janie could not have been more surprised by the change in the scenery. Instead of concrete streets, she was met with dirt roads. Instead of tall buildings, there were tiny shacks. She could not believe she was on the same landmass as the city. When did things get so lonely? Where were all of the people?

From Janie's bedroom window she could see a mountaintop. Her parents stared out at it every evening before the sun went down.

"Don't you think we should all climb to the top of that landform?" her dad asked. Janie quickly shook her head.

"No way, Dad," said Janie. "Why can't we just go back to the city? There is nothing to do here."

"Well, you wouldn't say that if you knew you were in charge of the hike!" said Mom. "I think you would find it quite interesting. And quite a challenge, too!"

1. What is the compound word in the first sentence?

_____

2. What are the two words that make up *landmass*?

_____

3. What are two compound words in the second paragraph?

_____

4. What is the compound word in the third paragraph? What do you think it means?

_____

Janie's Challenge

Continue the story from page 78. Use the words **countryside**, **mountaintop**, **landmass**, and **landform** in your story.

_____

_____

_____

_____

_____

_____

_____

_____

_____

_____

Earth's Beautiful Landforms

Earth has beautiful landforms, or natural features.
Choose one of Earth's landforms. Write about it.
Start each sentence with a letter from the word "landform."

L _____

A _____

N _____

D _____

F _____

O _____

R _____

M _____

Match Them Up!

Draw a line from a word in the left column to a word in the right column to make a compound word. Write the compound words you made on the lines below. Write a sentence for each one.

1.

land	side
tide	land
earth	pool
country	form
grass	quake

2. _____ _____

_____ _____

_____ _____

_____ _____

_____ _____

Complete the Sentences

Use the words from the word box below
to complete the sentences.

> grassland   tidepool   landform
>
> countryside   whirlpool
>
> earthquake   landmass   mountaintop

1. Giraffes and zebras may be found on the _____ of Africa.

2. The giant _____ is so big it can be seen from an airplane.

3. An _____ can be so powerful that it knocks books off the shelves.

4. I like living in the _____.

5. Tiny crabs and fish may live in a _____.

6. Sometimes the moving water of a _____ can be powerful.

7. It is not easy to climb up a _____.

8. What is your favorite kind of _____?

Compound Word Scramble

Unscramble each compound word below.

1. eeaakuqrht   _____

2. lsasnadm   _____

3. lwohoiprl   _____

4. yuoiesdtcnr   _____

5. potniatnuom   _____

6. ooeidtlp   _____

7. mlarondf   _____

8. dgnraassl   _____

Let's Go Over That Again

Review. Answer each question below.

1. The different features of earth have been given the name
_____.
  a. landform
  b. earthquake
  c. whirlpool

2. A place that is home to some living things during low tides on the beach is called a _____.
  a. grassland
  b. mountaintop
  c. tidepool

3. The top part of a mountain is called a _____.
  a. countryside
  b. mountaintop
  c. whirlpool

4. Part of the land that is scenic and not built up is called the
_____.
  a. countryside
  b. grassland
  c. landmass

5. A large, open area of country that is covered with grass is called a
_____.

    a. mountaintop
    b. grassland
    c. whirlpool

6. _____ is the name given to a sudden shaking of the
ground.
    a. landmass
    b. whirlpool
    c. earthquake

7. An area of water that quickly moves in a circle is called a
_____.

    a. whirlpool
    b. landmass
    c. tidepool

8. A large body of land is called a _____.
    a. mountaintop
    b. earthquake
    c. landmass

Word Search

There are eight words hidden in the puzzle. Use the definitions below to help you find them. Then write the words next to their meanings.

```
R  E  N  A  O  R  G  U  B  N
G  A  R  E  B  W  M  C  K  E
T  C  W  I  O  L  D  H  E  T
M  R  A  P  P  L  Y  A  V  Y
L  E  R  T  N  W  E  R  O  T
L  A  E  S  T  O  I  M  L  R
I  Q  U  K  P  A  U  N  E  F
K  U  I  V  A  N  C  P  O  H
S  G  L  A  N  C  E  K  N  E
```

1. a unit of land _____

2. to make a formal request _____

3. to strike _____

4. attractiveness, niceness _____

5. to look quickly _____

6. to moan _____

7. gentle _____

8. ability _____

Luis's Crop

Read the story. Then answer the questions below.

Luis was about to harvest his first crop of corn. In the spring he had planted an acre of corn behind his farmhouse. He had high hopes for the crops. But he wasn't quite sure if he had the skill to grow a crop.

Luis worked harder than he had ever worked before. He would groan every morning as he woke up. He had to water the crops and pull weeds. But he never complained after that first groan of the morning. He would quickly jump out of the bed. Then he would attack the weeds and do the watering.

Once in a while, Luis would have to apply a fertilizer to the crops. The crops grew faster with the fertilizer. And that's what Luis was looking for—fast-growing corn!

Finally, his hard work paid off. Anyone who drove by the farm could see Luis's hard work. With just a glance, they could see the tallest corn in the county. Luis had turned an acre of land into a harvest of his dreams.

1. What does the word **acre** refer to in paragraph 1?
   a. a type of corn   **b.** an amount of land   **c.** a season of the year

2. What word means the same as **skill**?
   a. tools   **b.** money   **c.** ability

3. What does the word **groan** tell you about how Luis felt when he woke up each morning?
   a. He was happy.   **b.** He was unhappy.   **c.** He was surprised.

4. What does the word **apply** mean in paragraph 3?
   a. to put on   **b.** to take off   **c.** to discover

Crossword Time!

Solve the crossword puzzle.

apply   attack   charm   meek

skill   glance   groan   acre

Across

1. rhymes with **try**
2. rhymes with **harm**
4. rhymes with **hill**
5. rhymes with **stone**

Down

1. rhymes with **back**
3. rhymes with **week**
5. rhymes with **chance**
6. rhymes with **shaker**

A Poem About Meek

The word **meek** means quiet, or gentle. Choose an animal that you think of as meek. Write a poem about that animal. Your poem should describe how the animal is meek.

_____

_____

_____

_____

_____

_____

_____

_____

Scrambled Words

Unscramble each word below.

1. ylpap _____

2. norag _____

3. llski _____

4. hmrac _____

5. tatakc _____

6. keem _____

7. acengl _____

8. reac _____

How Charming!

Look at each use of the word **charm**.
Write **correct** or **incorrect** under each sentence.

1. The painting has a lot of style and **charm**.

_____

2. You are very **charming** when you smile and laugh.

_____

3. The man acts like a **charmist** to get what he wants.

_____

4. Becky is more **charmer** than Abby.

_____

5. Mom read a **charmling** little story to my class.

_____

6. A handmade painting is more **charming** than a photocopy.

_____

Let's Go Over That Again

Review. Answer each question below.

1. An acre is a _____.
   a. unit of land
   b. unit of liquid
   c. unit of weight

2. When you glance at something, you _____.
   a. look carefully
   b. look quickly
   c. look with excitement

3. Another word for charm is _____.
   a. horror
   b. confusion
   c. delight

4. Another word for skill is _____.
   a. ability
   b. anger
   c. attack

5. A groan is a kind of a _____.
    a. person
    b. noise
    c. measurement

6. An attack is an act that is _____.
    a. angry
    b. funny
    c. unusual

7. When you apply for something, you are answering a _____.
    a. request
    b. promise
    c. shout

8. Someone who is meek can be described as _____.
    a. weak
    b. strong
    c. funny

The Dictionary of America

Look at the dictionary entries below. The words are out of order!
List the words in the correct alphabetical order below.

pres•i•dent *noun*   An elected head of a society or other group

lib•er•ty *noun*   The state of being free within a society or group

vote. *noun*   A formal choice between groups or actions

coun•try *noun*   A nation with its own government

his•to•ry *noun*   The study of events of the past

pick•et *noun*   A protest about something that tries to persuade other people

cit•i•zen *noun*   A person who legally lives in a town or city

ter•ri•to•ry *noun*   An area of land run by a government

_____

_____

_____

_____

_____

_____

_____

My Country, Your Country

Read the story. Circle the correct answer to each question.

Marcos moved to the United States from Cuba three years ago. Since then, Marcos has been very busy. He has been learning about life in this country. He has been learning to speak the language. He wants to become a citizen just as soon as he is old enough.

Marcos has a lot to learn about the history of the United States. He knows about the fight for liberty. He is learning about how the territory has grown. He can name every state by heart.

He also knows that it is alright for Americans to hold picket signs. If you don't agree with something in this country, it is fine to say so. That's what liberty is all about! As soon as Marcos is old enough, he hopes to be able to vote for the president.

1. What country did Marcos and his family move to?
   a. Brazil   **b.** United States

2. What is a **citizen**?
   a. someone who is a legal member   **b.** someone who lives someplace

3. What does **history** mean?
   a. the future   **b.** the past

4. What does Marcos think liberty is all about?
   a. doing what you are told   **b.** doing what you want

5. What does it mean if you are carrying a picket sign?
   a. you agree with something   **b.** you disagree with something

6. What does **vote** mean?
   a. to make a choice   **b.** to make someone angry

7. What does Marcos mean by **territory**?
   a. land   **b.** people

Word Search

There are eight words hidden in the puzzle. Use the definitions below to help you find them. Then write the words next to their meanings.

```
T  E  R  R  I  T  O  R  Y  M
N  C  E  P  I  C  K  E  T  A
E  O  G  H  J  E  D  S  A  X
D  U  B  L  H  S  I  F  E  U
I  N  Y  C  I  T  I  Z  E  N
S  T  C  O  S  B  O  T  T  J
E  R  K  P  T  P  E  G  O  X
R  Y  W  L  O  W  S  R  V  E
P  A  B  T  R  E  W  M  T  R
L  K  O  U  Y  G  G  E  U  Y
```

1. a person who lives in a state or country _____

2. nation _____

3. events that happened in the past _____

4. freedom _____

5. to protest or go on strike _____

6. leader of a country _____

7. area of land _____

8. to make a formal choice _____

Fill in the Blanks

Use words from the word box to fill in the blanks below.

citizens   vote   history

country   liberty

    In 1776, the American colonies fought in the American Revolution. They fought against England for their _____. The colonies were tired of being ruled by a king who was thousands of miles away. The colonists had no rights of their own. They were not able to _____ for the rules and laws that governed them. And they were not _____ of England, either. What the colonists wanted was to form their own _____. They wanted to be free from the king's rule. These decisions made our country's _____ what it is today. Thanks, colonists, for fighting for our freedom!

Crossword Time!

Solve the crossword puzzle.

citizen   country   history   liberty

picket   president   territory   vote

Across
1. freedom
3. an area of land
4. member of a country
6. leader of a country

Down
2. to protest against something
5. the past
7. a nation that is run by a government
8. a formal choice

What Does Liberty Mean?

Draw a picture below that shows what the word **liberty** means to you.
Then write a caption to explain your picture.

_____

_____

Let's Go Over That Again

Review. Fill in the blanks below with words from the word box.

citizen   country   history

liberty   picket

president   territory   vote

1. When you have freedom, you have _____.

2. When you disagree with something, you can join a _____ against that thing.

3. Land owned by a government is called a _____.

4. Things that happened in our past are called our _____.

5. The person who leads our country is the _____.

6. When you choose which person you want to lead us, you _____ for him or her.

7. Someone who legally lives in a country or state is called a _____.

8. The United States of America is a _____ in North America.

Match Them Up

Draw a line from the word on the left to the definition on the right.

1. **country**

2. **history**

3. **liberty**

4. **vote**

5. **territory**

6. **citizen**

7. **president**

8. **picket**

a. the state of being free within a society or group

b. an area of land run by a government

c. a person who legally lives in a town or city

d. the study of events of the past

e. an elected head of a society or other group

f. a nation with its own government

g. a protest about something that tries to persuade other people

h. a formal choice between groups or action

Suffixes, Suffixes

A **suffix** is an ending of a word.
Underline the suffix of each word below.

cheerful

friendly

rested

hopeless

wishful

jumping

caring

greatest

properly

mostly

gladly

presently

grateful

fearless

Suffixes That Compare

Circle and write in **–er** or **–est** to correctly complete each sentence.

1. James is the great___ pitcher in his baseball league.   er   est

2. We walked fast___ when the weather was colder.   er   est

3. Jake's grades were high___ than Monica's grades.   er   est

4. Are you the smart___ student in the class?   er   est

5. I think you should buy the small___ gift they have.   er   est

6. Leah's hair is straight___ than Julia's.   er   est

7. Today's test was the hard___ one I have ever taken!   er   est

Who Does That Job?

The suffixes **–er** and **–or** can mean "a person who." The suffixes can be put on the end of verbs to make them into nouns. Write the correct suffix at the end of each word. Then use the new word in a sentence.

1. teach_____ _____

2. design_____ _____

3. edit_____ _____

4. conduct_____ _____

5. sculpt_____ _____

6. photograph_____ _____

7. sing_____ _____

8. instruct_____ _____

9. counsel_____ _____

10. report_____ _____

More Work That People Do

Underline the suffix of each person's job.
Then write what you think that person does.

librarian _____

writer _____

geologist _____

scientist _____

mail carrier _____

dentist _____

surgeon _____

governor _____

welder _____

dietician _____

musician _____

actor _____

Choosing Suffixes

Choose the correct ending for the word to make the sentence make sense.

1. We had a wonder___ time at the movies last night.   **ly**   **ful**

2. We neat___ hung our coats on the backs of our chairs.   **ly**   **ful**

3. Mom kind___ bought us popcorn and drinks.   **ly**   **ful**

4. Dad brought a pocket___ of change for the video games.   **ly**   **ful**

5. My sister excited___ played before the movie started.   **ly**   **ful**

6. We were all perfect___ happy with our family night out.   **ly**   **ful**

Choose More Suffixes

Choose the correct ending for the word to make the sentence make sense.

1. Studying for the test was pain____.   ness   less

2. My biggest problem was that neat____ counts!   ness   less

3. I have messy handwriting, but I am not care____.   ness   less

4. I hope the teacher will show some kind____!   ness   less

5. After school, I will feel great____.   ness   less

6. But I do have to clean my room until it is spot____.   ness   less

7. I know it is use____ to complain!   ness   less

Guitar Lessons

Read the story. Fill in the blanks with the words from the word box.

fearless   foolish   dedicated   careful

happily   adventurous   excitedly

Johnny was ready for a new and _____ journey. He was going to take guitar lessons. He was _____ to make the lessons at a time when he would not be tired. He took the lessons before school. His mom thought it was a little _____ to get up so early. Johnny _____ traded sleep for the chance to learn how to play guitar.

Johnny went to his lessons every day before school. Then he ran home and _____ practiced until dinner. Others might be afraid to make mistakes, but not Johnny. He was a _____ performer. He played for anyone who would listen.

Is there anything that you are so _____ to?

Making Words

Draw a line from the word on the left
to the suffix that goes with it on the right.

1. friend   ful

2. fear   est

3. teach   ly

4. great   er

Write a suffix that can go with each word below.

5. perfect_____

6. wonder_____

7. use_____

8. try_____

9. nice_____

Let's Go Over That Again

Review. Answer each question below.

1. A suffix that means "one who" is _____.
   a. -ing
   b. -or
   c. -est

2. A suffix that compares two things is _____.
   a. -less
   b. -ness
   c. -er

3. A suffix that means "the most" is _____.
   a. -est
   b. -less
   c. -ist

4. A suffix that means "without" is _____.
   a. -est
   b. -less
   c. -ist

5. A suffix that shows action is _____.
   a. -or
   b. -ing
   c. -ly

6. Endless means _____.
  a. without end
  b. one who ends
  c. the act of ending

7. A scientist is _____.
  a. without science
  b. one who studies science
  c. full of science

8. Wonderful means _____.
  a. one who wonders
  b. without wonder
  c. full of wonder

9. Fearful means _____.
  a. without fear
  b. full of fear
  c. one who has fear

10. Nicest means_____.
  a. one who is nice
  b. the most nice of all
  c. nicer than some

Word Search

There are seven words hidden in the puzzle. Use the definitions below to help you find them. Then write the words next to their meanings.

```
B  L  D  O  I  U  G  D  R  S
L  B  O  T  H  U  N  D  E  R
I  R  B  K  O  Y  Z  T  S  S
Z  E  F  T  U  R  I  O  M  E
Z  D  I  M  U  H  N  E  O  C
A  N  X  E  V  M  Y  A  G  E
R  U  T  D  R  E  K  D  A
D  H  W  B  K  Y  O  N  X  O
A  T  M  O  S  P  H  E  R  E
H  U  R  R  I  C  A  N  E  N
```

1. heavy air _____

2. strong storm with heavy winds _____

3. storm with rotating winds _____

4. the air around us _____

5. storm with heavy snow _____

6. fog or haze _____

7. rumbling sound that comes after lightning _____

Know Your Weather

Read the story. Then answer the questions below.

To learn about the weather, you must learn about the atmosphere. The atmosphere is the layer of gases that surround our Earth. Other planets have atmospheres, too. On Earth, the atmosphere makes our weather.

Rain is moisture in the atmosphere that thickens and falls to the ground. When there is a lot of water vapor in the atmosphere, the air is called humid. Sometimes these weather conditions are calm and still. Other times they are violent and strong.

A hurricane is a severe storm with very high winds. Many hurricanes start over the ocean. They can reach land and cause much damage.

A tornado is a violent, rotating cloud in the shape of a funnel. Tornadoes start quickly and can cause a lot of damage to property. A tornado can be spotted in the distance. These dangerous storms often occur in flat areas, such as in the middle section of the United States.

1. Which word has the closest meaning to **atmosphere**?

   a. air   **b.** storm   **c.** tornado

2. Which type of weather causes a funnel-shaped cloud?

   a. rain   **b.** hurricane   **c.** tornado

3. What is humid air?

_____

4. What kinds of weather can cause damage to property?

_____

Crossword Time!

Use the clues below to solve the crossword puzzle.

Across
1. the layer of gases around earth or another planet
4. a lot of water vapor in the air
5. violent, rotating winds in a funnel-shaped cloud

Down
2. crashing sound that is heard after lightning strikes
3. a fog or haze in the atmosphere
6. a storm with violent winds
7. a severe snowstorm

Weather Word Scramble

Unscramble the words below. Then use each word in a sentence.

1. ogms

_____

_____

2. oodantr

_____

_____

3. zzradilb

_____

_____

4. dimhu

_____

_____

5. iaeurhrcn

_____

_____

6. moreepshta

_____

_____

7. nreduht

_____

_____

Weather Feelings

Fill in each blank with a word from the word box.

humid   hurricane   tornado

atmosphere   blizzard   smog   thunder

1.   I feel great when the _____ is clear.

2.   I shiver with cold when I am in the middle of a _____.

3.   I would be scared if I ever saw the funnel cloud of a _____ coming my way!

4.   I worry about damaging winds when I hear about a _____.

5.   I think the air can look dirty when there is _____.

6.   I feel hot and sticky when the air is _____.

7.   I cover my ears when I hear loud _____.

Weather Experiences

Choose a storm or weather experience that you remember.
Write about how it made you feel. Use descriptive words.
Draw a picture to go with your story.

_____

_____

_____

_____

_____

Let's Go Over That Again

Review. Answer the questions below.

1. How is a tornado different from a hurricane?

_____

_____

2. What is an **atmosphere**?

_____

_____

3. What is the word for a haze or fog in the air?

_____

4. What kind of storm happens most often during the winter in a cold climate?

_____

5. What kind of air has the most water vapor, or moisture, in it?

_____

6. All planets are surrounded by an _____.
   a. thunder
   b. atmosphere
   c. blizzard

7. When the air is hard to see through, you may be looking at _____.
   a. atmosphere
   b. thunder
   c. smog

8. A storm with a lot of snow is a _____.
   a. blizzard
   b. tornado
   c. hurricane

9. The sound that happens after lightning strikes is called _____.
   a. thunder
   b. smog
   c. humid

10. Sticky, wet weather in the summer is often called _____.
   a. tornado
   b. atmosphere
   c. humid

Grammar Words

Read the definitions of the grammar words below.
Then put the dictionary words in alphabetical order.

noun a person, place, thing, or idea

adjective a word that describes a noun

verb an action word

adverb a word that describes a verb or adjective

pronoun a word used in place of a noun or noun phrase

article a word that introduces a phrase, such as *the*, *a*, or *an*

preposition a word that comes before a noun to give information of time, place, or direction, such as: *on*, *over*, *under*, or *in*

paragraph a section of writing dealing with a single idea

_____

_____

_____

_____

_____

_____

_____

Word Search

There are eight words hidden in the puzzle. Use the definitions below to help you find them. Then write the words next to their meanings.

```
A   D   J   E   C   T   I   V   E   S   V
S   K   I   X   A   O   C   N   P   E   U
G   R   H   S   R   D   N   D   S   W   R
O   H   W   N   T   G   V   P   R   S   D
K   P   S   U   I   O   E   E   U   L   B
O   A   R   O   C   B   R   L   R   I   J
P   R   T   N   L   O   B   H   E   B   T
R   G   J   O   E   J   C   F   P   I   O
E   A   K   R   N   E   B   Y   K   Q   E
P   R   E   P   O   S   I   T   I   O   N
A   A   U   M   U   L   Q   T   R   V   O
E   P   W   C   N   B   S   F   C   X   A
```

1. describing word _____

2. modifies a word by place or time _____

3. comes before a noun: the, a, an _____

4. person, place, thing, or idea _____

5. group of related sentences _____

6. describes time or location: after, on, below _____

7. replaces a noun: she, he, it _____

8. action word _____

Crossword Time!

Use the clues below to solve the crossword puzzle.

Across

1. word that comes before a noun to tell about time, place, or direction

4. word that introduces a phrase, such as *the*, *a*, or *an*

5. word that describes a noun

Down

2. a word used in place of a noun

3. section of writing dealing with a single idea

6. action word

7. person, place, thing, or idea

8. word that describes a verb or adjective

What Kind of Word Is It?

Write the part of speech for each underlined word.

article   noun   verb   preposition

adverb   pronoun   adjective

1. The <u>dog</u> jumped onto my lap and spilled my drink. _____

2. I sprang to my feet <u>immediately</u>! _____

3. "Down, Fido," I <u>yelled</u>. _____

4. I looked down at my <u>wet</u> shirt. _____

5. Fido frowned and walked sadly <u>down</u> the hall. _____

6. Even when he was bad <u>he</u> was the cutest dog ever. _____

7. "Aw, poor Fido," I said as I went to get <u>a</u> new shirt. _____

What's That Word Called?

Circle the word in each sentence that matches
the part of speech on the left.

1. verb   I have to swim for a half hour at practice today.

2. adjective   The coach loves my new goggles.

3. article   We cannot get used to the cold water today.

4. noun   Swimmers usually adjust pretty quickly.

5. preposition   I can't wait to put that towel around my body!

6. adverb   I have to wait patiently until practice is over.

7. pronoun   We are having fun, even though it is cold today!

Now YOU Think of the Words

Write examples of each kind of word in the box.
Give as many examples as you can of each.

Noun

Verb

Adjective

Article

Preposition

Adverb

Pronoun

Write a paragraph.

Let's Go Over That Again

Review. Answer each question below.

1. A word that shows action is a _____.
   a. verb
   b. article
   c. pronoun

2. A word that describes a noun is a _____.
   a. noun
   b. verb
   c. adjective

3. A word that names a person, place, thing, or idea is a _____.
   a. verb
   b. noun
   c. preposition

4. A section of writing about a single idea is a _____.
   a. preposition
   b. paragraph
   c. pronoun

5. A word that describes a verb or adjective is a _____.
   a. pronoun
   b. adverb
   c. noun

Review. Answer each question below with a part of speech.

6. The word **justice** is a _____.

7. The word **she** is a _____.

8. The word **leap** is a _____.

9. The word **creative** is a _____.

10. The word **creatively** is a _____.

11. The word **the** is a _____.

12. The word **into** is a _____.

BONUS: Write a sentence that uses an article, pronoun,
noun, verb, adjective, adverb, and preposition.

_____

_____

_____

Multiple Meaning Words

Some words have more than one meaning.
Circle the word in each sentence that has more than one meaning.
Then write a sentence that uses another meaning for the word.

1. We like to treat people with respect.

_____

2. I could not bear it if I made someone sad!

_____

3. Can you scale a wall like a superhero?

_____

4. If you season that food a little more it will be too spicy for me.

_____

5. Today is a great day to loaf around the house.

_____

6. I hope my problem did not hamper your plans for this evening.

_____

7. If you lift the hatch in the floor you will see where I hide
some extra change.

_____

8. The new girl hails from the south.

_____

Word Search

There are eight words hidden in the puzzle. Use the definitions below to help you find them. Then write the words next to their meanings.

```
L  R  A  C  K  E  T  U  K
T  F  A  R  D  N  G  T  S
U  P  U  Z  Z  L  E  G  E
G  H  A  R  V  N  S  R  A
L  A  E  S  U  Y  F  A  S
S  Q  U  A  S  H  G  D  O
B  D  V  E  S  N  T  E  N
S  N  L  I  P  O  U  N  D
H  A  M  P  E  R  O  L  W
```

1. to give a score _____

2. basket for laundry _____

3. to give from one person to another _____

4. to bang or hammer something _____

5. confuse _____

6. noise _____

7. to add spices to something _____

8. a vegetable _____

Jessie's Kitchen

Read the story. Then answer the questions below.

Many people can gain a pound simply by looking at Chef Jessie's kitchen. It is the most amazing kitchen in the world, many people say.
Jessie is the kind of cook that will season every dish to the tastes of his guests. He will never loaf around the kitchen. Instead, he will make you a loaf of your favorite kind of bread! He hatches a new plan for his menu every day. He will use summer squash for an appetizer. Then he will squash some beans into a paste or a dip.

People sit on the stoop of Jessie's restaurant for hours waiting for it to open. They wait even longer to meet Jessie in person. But Jessie would not stoop to such a level. He does not want to meet any of his customers. He simply wants to know what they like to eat. And then he cooks for them. Some people think this is a rude attitude to take with the public. But no one could bear to tell him to his face! What if he decided not to cook for them? That would be a real tragedy!

1. What multiple-meaning word can be found in the first sentence of the passage?

_____

2. What are the two meanings of **loaf** in the second paragraph?

_____   _____

3. What are the two meanings of **squash** in the second paragraph?

_____   _____

4. What are the two meanings of **stoop** in the last paragraph?

_____   _____

130

Find the Other Meaning

Read each sentence and its underlined multiple-meaning word. Then write a new sentence that uses the other meaning of the underlined word.

1. The kids love to have a healthy <u>treat</u> during snack time.

_____

2. The <u>bear</u> went over the mountain to see what it could see.

_____

3. The ducks may <u>hatch</u> from their eggs by the end of the week.

_____

4. If you want to know how much you weigh, get on the <u>scale</u>.

_____

5. Logan kicked the ball about a <u>yard</u> farther than Carrie did.

_____

A Multiple-Meaning Poem

Write a poem using the multiple-meaning words in the word box. You do not have to use two meanings for the word, but try it for a challenge!

bear   treat   hatch   yard

_____

_____

_____

_____

_____

_____

_____

_____

Draw Multiple Meanings!

Draw a picture to illustrate this sentence
with multiple-meaning words.

The bear could not bear to take food from the campers.

Let's Go Over That Again

Review. Find the answer that shows another
meaning for the underlined word.

1. A fish <u>scale</u> is like dry, flaky skin.

   a. a tool for measuring weight

   b. a place where people eat

   c. a big balloon

2. Sarah took the banana bread <u>loaf</u> out of the oven.

   a. to be lazy

   b. a drink

   c. a tool for baking food

3. Doug is so kind he would not even <u>squash</u> a bug.

   a. a type of computer

   b. a type of vegetable

   c. a type of road

4. You may have to <u>stoop</u> down to get through the tiny doorway.

   a. movement

   b. front steps

   c. swimming pool

5. Your <u>yard</u> looks so pretty in the summer.

    a. a vehicle

    b. a unit of weight

    c. a unit of length

6. I will <u>treat</u> you as well as you treat others.

    a. a movie

    b. a snack

    c. homework

7. You need a special <u>pass</u> to get into the museum.

    a. to get a high grade

    b. to talk to a friend

    c. to understand

8. I don't mean to <u>puzzle</u> you, but I don't know where my keys are.

    a. a game

    b. a book

    c. a shoe

Compound Words

A **compound word** is a word made of two smaller words. You can try to find the meaning of a compound word by looking at its smaller parts. Make a compound word from two words. Write the word on the line.

1. base + ball =

_____

2. dog + house =

_____

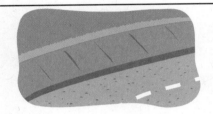

3. side + walk =

_____

4. cup + cake =

_____

5. snow + storm =

_____

6. butter + fly =

_____

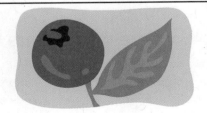

7. blue + berry =

_____

8. down + stairs =

_____

Find the Meaning of the Compound Words

Circle each compound word below.
Then write what you think the word means.

1. Sparky needs a new horseshoe on his feet.

_____

2. If you see a rattlesnake, stay away!

_____

3. Has anyone seen my hairbrush?

_____

4. Look in the mailbox for the letter.

_____

5. You can order a cheeseburger at the restaurant.

_____

6. Let's make some popcorn!

_____

7. Go hang up your raincoat.

_____

Make a Compound Word

Circle each word that makes a compound word
to complete each sentence.

1. You should not walk to the park bare____.   foot   house

2. Can you meet me out____ in the garden?   play   side

3. I like to play foot____ with my friends.   ball   bake

4. I would like to be a cow____ when I grow up.   flag   boy

5. We can get honey from the ____hive.   bird   bee

6. A tiny ____bug landed on my arm.   truck   lady

7. Who will put the flag up the ____pole today?   pole   flag

8. A space____ will take off for Mars.   boat   ship

Word Search

There are six compound words hidden in the puzzle. Use the definitions below to help you find them. Then write the words next to their meanings.

```
H  G  T  A  S  K  O  M  H
S  C  A  R  E  C  R  O  W
I  T  G  R  A  B  U  C  R
F  R  D  O  W  E  A  P  R
D  E  X  W  E  D  T  I  U
L  E  E  H  E  R  D  O  P
O  T  L  E  D  O  M  W  P
G  O  A  A  S  O  P  C  R
W  P  S  D  I  M  G  E  J
```

1. head of an arrow _____

2. golden colored fish _____

3. top of a tree _____

4. weed that grows in the sea _____

5. room with a bed _____

6. object for scaring crows in a field _____

Match Up Words

Draw a line from the word in the left column to the word in the right column to make a compound word.

egg	house
farm	room
moon	corn
bed	shell
pop	melon
water	light
meat	bow
rain	ball

Creating Compound Words

Add a new word to the end of each word to make a compound.

1. camp

_____

2. scare

_____

3. cup

_____

4. bath

_____

5. fire

_____

6. volley

_____

7. junk

_____

8. gold

_____

9. Write three sentences using the words you made.

_____

_____

_____

Dave's Goldfish Farm

Read the story. Then answer the questions below.

Most farmers tend to cows or chickens. But Dave has always been a little bit different. He is a goldfish farmer. He doesn't have a farmhouse. He doesn't collect eggs at sunrise. Dave raises goldfish so they can be used in beautiful ponds all around the country.

When he was growing up, his bedroom walls were covered with pictures of fish. He wanted to live underwater! But then he learned that would not be possible for a human. So he quickly decided that he would raise fish for a living.

He feeds his fish every morning. He cares for them in the afternoon. And he thinks about them all night long. Dave was born to raise fish!

It's always hard for Dave to say goodbye to his fish once he sells them. But he knows there are always more swimming in the pond in the backyard!

1. How many compound words were used in the passage? _____

2. Write them on the lines.

_____

_____

Illustrate a Compound Word

Choose two words from the word box below.
Make your own nonsense compound word. Then illustrate it!

mail   junk   yard   horse   egg   shoe
shell   brush   room   star   rattle
light   snake   moon   space

Let's Go Over That Again

Review. Write your own definition for each compound word.

1. What is an <u>eggshell</u>?

_____

_____

2. What is a <u>bedroom</u>?

_____

_____

3. What is <u>sunshine</u>?

_____

_____

4. What is a <u>doghouse</u>?

_____

_____

5. What is a <u>snowstorm</u>?

_____

_____

Review. Make a compound word out of the words below.
Then write a sentence using the word.

6. shoe + lace =   _____

_____

7. straw + berry =   _____

_____

8. card + board =   _____

_____

9. flag + pole =   _____

_____

10. star + light =   _____

_____

11. space + ship =   _____

_____

12. broom + stick =   _____

_____

Sayings and Expressions

There are different kinds of sayings that people use to make their language more interesting. Many sayings and expressions compare two or more things. Some of them use the words **like** or **as** to make the comparisons. Others do not. Read the sentences below. Underline the sayings or expressions.

1. When I looked outside it was raining cats and dogs.

2. My grandmother always says that time is a thief.

3. The dog's fur looked as shiny as an apple.

4. Mark will be in a world of hurt if he doesn't do his homework on time.

5. A famous writer once wrote that all the world is a stage.

6. Mom said she's been working like a dog all afternoon.

Draw an Expression

Have you ever heard the expression "I'm as busy as a bee?"
In the space below, draw a picture of yourself as busy as a bee.
Then write a caption that uses the expression.

_____

My New Kitty

Read the story. Then answer the questions below.

My new cat Nibbles is as cute as a button. The bad part is, she is also as tricky as a fox. She gets into trouble at every turn. But I can't really get mad at her. All she has to do is look up at me with her big blue eyes. Nibbles has eyes that melt my heart.

Mom thinks that if Nibbles does not learn to behave she could be up the creek without a paddle. I know that I can train my kitty to be good, though. She seems to be as smart as a whip! She remembers anything I say. Her mind is like a steel trap.

So I think that Nibbles is just acting like a kitty when she misbehaves. And how can I blame her? She is just taking life by the horns!

1. What does the saying in the first sentence mean?

_____

2. Why do people use the saying "tricky as a fox?"

_____

3. What is another saying from paragraph one?

_____

4. Rewrite the first sentence of paragraph two without the phrase, "up the creek without a paddle."

_____

_____

_____

Illustrate Your Favorite

Think about the sayings used in the passage on page 148.
Choose one that you like best and illustrate it below.
Below the picture, write the sentence that you are illustrating.

Silly Similes

A **simile** is a saying that compares two unlike things using the words **like** or **as**. The saying "as free as a bird" is a simile. Draw a line to match the first and second part of the similes below.

1. happy   as a pancake

2. flat   as a wolf

3. dry   as a turtle

4. sharp   as a cucumber

5. hungry   as a clown

6. slow   as nails

7. cool   as a bone

Write Your Own Sayings

Write your own story or poem. Be sure to use at least three sayings, or expressions, in your work. Underline the sayings that you use.

_____

_____

_____

_____

_____

_____

_____

_____

_____

_____

_____

_____

Let's Go Over That Again

Review. Answer each question below.

1. What does the saying "clear as a bell" refer to?
   a. time
   b. sound
   c. sight

2. What does the saying "he is a pig" mean?
   a. He is messy.
   b. He is clean.
   c. He is small.

3. What does the saying "a feverish pace" mean?
   a. a high speed
   b. a low speed
   c. a sick feeling

4. What does the saying "I could eat a horse" mean?
   a. I am at home.
   b. I am very hungry.
   c. I like to eat horses.

5. What does the saying "you are a bottomless pit" mean?
   a. You can eat a lot.
   b. You can talk a lot.
   c. You can sing a lot.

Review. Choose the ending of the phrase
to make a simile that makes sense.

6. You are as sharp as a _____.
    a. knife
    b. pillow
    c. pet

7. You are as delicate as a _____.
    a. rock
    b. flower
    c. brick

8. You are as loud as a _____.
    a. mouse
    b. person
    c. lion

9. You are as straight as an _____.
    a. acorn
    b. apple
    c. arrow

10. You are as slow as _____.
    a. a snail
    b. a cheetah
    c. a train

A Technology Dictionary

The dictionary entries below are out of order. Read the meanings for the words. Then put the words in alphabetical order at the bottom of the page.

net•work   a number of computers connected together to share information

down•load   to get a file from another computer or over a network and to save it on your own computer

da•ta•base   an organized collection of information that can be sorted and analyzed

soft•ware   the programs that run on a computer

mem•o•ry   temporary storage space on a computer

gig•a•byte   unit of measurement about equal to a billion bytes, or bits of information

pe•riph•er•al   a device separate from a computer, usually connected to the computer by a cable

hard•ware   parts of a computer system that can be touched, such as keyboard, mouse, and monitor

brows•er   a software system that allows you to search the Internet

1. _____ 2. _____

3. _____ 4. _____

5. _____ 6. _____

7. _____ 8. _____

9. _____

Technology Words

There are nine words hidden in the puzzle. Use the definitions below to help you find them. Then write the words next to their meanings.

```
M  E  M  O  R  Y  H  O  P  S
N  B  R  O  W  S  E  R  E  O
K  F  U  L  V  X  D  W  R  F
O  P  T  H  K  E  A  Q  I  T
Y  B  D  Y  N  L  T  R  P  W
D  O  W  N  L  O  A  D  H  A
I  R  W  P  B  Y  B  E  E  R
E  R  A  W  D  R  A  H  R  E
A  S  J  O  V  T  S  S  A  W
U  K  R  O  W  T  E  N  L  O
G  I  G  A  B  Y  T  E  L  K
```

1. computer program that allows you to search the Internet

   _____

2. device attached to a computer _____

3. to move data from one computer to another _____

4. computer programs _____

5. computer equipment or machines _____

6. large unit of computer information _____

7. arrangement of computer connections _____

8. computer's power to remember information _____

9. collection of data _____

Technology Word Scramble

Unscramble the technology words below.

1. ggbyetai   _____

2. yoermm   _____

3. roeswrb   _____

4. doaldnwo   _____

5. daerwarh   _____

6. krtwoen   _____

7. hrelahiperp   _____

8. aaaedtbs   _____

9. wfstreao   _____

Connected to the World

Read the story. Fill in the blanks in the paragraph
with the words from the word box.

browser	database	download
gigabytes	hardware	software
memory	network	peripherals

Ever since Jason was old enough to walk and talk, he loved his parents' computer. He tried to touch the keyboard and other _____ whenever he could. He would touch the wires that went with the _____ on the side of the computer.

His dad used to sit him on his lap in front of the screen when he was tiny. They would use a _____ to search the Internet. They would look for toddler games online. They would _____ puzzles and coloring sheets for Jason to play with.

Today Jason knows almost everything there is to know about computers. He does not have many _____ on his hand-me-down computer. But he can hook up to his dad's _____ and be part of the family computers. He thinks he may even know more than his parents do about the computer!

Technology Poem

Write a poem about technology. Use one of the letters of the word **gigabyte** to start each line of your poem.

G _____

I _____

G _____

A _____

B _____

Y _____

T _____

E _____

More Technology Fun

Write more about technology. Try another poem. Use one of the letters of the word **download** to start each line of your poem.

D_____

O_____

W_____

N_____

L_____

O_____

A_____

D_____

Let's Go Over That Again

Review. Draw a line from the word on the left
to the correct meaning on the right.

1. peripheral

a. a number of computers connected together to share information

2. network

b. a software system that allows you to search the Internet

3. hardware

c. to get a file from another computer or over a network and to save it on your own computer

4. browser

d. a device separate from a computer, usually connected to the computer by a cable

5. download

e. parts of a computer system that can be touched, such as keyboard, mouse, and monitor

6. software

f. an organized collection of information that can be sorted and analyzed

7. database

g. temporary storage space on a computer

8. gigabyte

h. the programs that run on a computer

9. memory

i. unit of measure about equal to a billion bytes, or bits of information

Antonyms

Antonyms are words with opposite or near opposite meanings. **Hot** and **cold** are opposites. Draw a line to match the word on the left to its antonym on the right.

1. generous	rude
2. private	present
3. polite	maximum
4. occupied	stingy
5. absent	vacant
6. minimum	public
7. narrow	broad

Antonym Questions

Read each sentence. Fill in the blanks with the antonym of each underlined word.

1. Is the water <u>shallow</u>?

No, it is _____.   deep   dirty

2. Is the food <u>stale</u>?

No, it is _____.   hot   fresh

3. Was the man <u>absent</u>?

No, he was _____.   rude   present

4. Is the party <u>public</u>?

No, it is _____.   private   fun

5. Was the boat ride <u>gentle</u>?

No, it was _____.   rough   long

6. Is the animal <u>common</u>?

No, it is _____.   old   rare

Crossword Time!

Solve the crossword puzzle below.

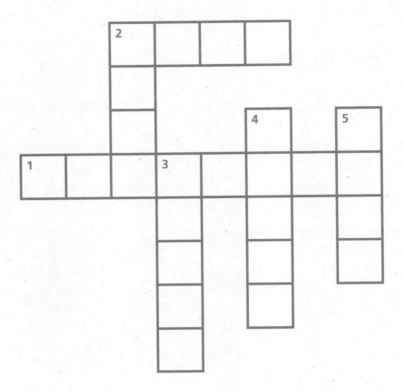

Across

1. antonym of **no one**

2. antonym of **low**

Down

2. antonym of **love**

3. antonym of **wrong**

4. antonym of **smooth**

5. antonym of **purchase**

Picture the Opposite

Write an antonym for each word.
Then draw a picture of it in the box.

empty _____

narrow _____

swift _____

inexpensive _____

flexible _____

tremendous _____

What's the Opposite?

Think of an antonym for each word on the left.
Then write a sentence using that antonym.

1. question _____

2. arrive _____

3. exhale _____

4. borrow _____

5. foolish _____

6. swift _____

7. joy _____

8. wise _____

Word Search

There are eight words hidden in the puzzle. Use the definitions below to help you find them. Then write the words next to their meanings.

```
E   C   T   J   S   C   D   H   L
D   A   N   G   E   R   O   U   S
O   L   D   W   A   L   W   B   A
K   M   U   V   I   P   N   G   F
T   C   P   A   L   L   D   U   E
W   G   N   U   O   Y   D   S   H
```

1. having lived for a short time _____

2. having lived for a long time _____

3. protected, not in danger _____

4. able to cause harm _____

5. not nervous _____

6. uncontrolled _____

7. toward the sky _____

8. toward the ground _____

On My Street

Read the story. Fill in the blanks using words from the box.

happy   country   hates

scarce   calm   empty

     I love my street. My sister disagrees with me because she _____ living here. I think the city is the best place to live, while she prefers the _____. In the city, stores and shops are abundant. In the country, they are much more _____. I would be miserable if I could not walk to my local shops. But it seems that my sister would be _____ without the stores.

     I like that the city is busy, but she would like it if things were _____. We are different in many ways. I like to see the restaurant tables full and bustling with people, and she likes it when they are _____ and quiet.

168

Word Scramble

Unscramble each set of antonyms below.

1. ccersa   tbdunana

_____   _____

2. tslo   nfuod

_____   _____

3. weobl   veabo

_____   _____

4. tis   andts

_____   _____

5. arhd   ysae

_____   _____

6. gtear   rrohelib

_____   _____

Let's Go Over That Again

Review. Choose the antonym for each word.

1. create
   a. bake
   b. destroy
   c. help

2. horrible
   a. great
   b. large
   c. calm

3. break
   a. scream
   b. talk
   c. repair

4. whisper
   a. sing
   b. scream
   c. talk

5. pull
   a. stop
   b. push
   c. drink

Review. Write the antonym for each word below.

6. sell   _____

7. city   _____

8. stand   _____

9. expensive   _____

10. swift   _____

Write your own pairs of antonyms below.

11. _____   _____

12. _____   _____

13. _____   _____

14. _____   _____

Health Words

Some words have to do with your health.
Put the health words below in alphabetical order.

in•fec•tion	the growth of tiny, harmful organisms in a body
vi•rus	a kind of organism that makes people sick
germ	tiny organism, may cause disease
pre•scrip•tion	medicine given by a doctor
vac•cine	a substance that protects against disease
sur•ger•y	the act of a doctor opening the body and correcting a problem inside the body
treat•ment	the action taken to make a person feel better

1. _____

2. _____

3. _____

4. _____

5. _____

6. _____

7. _____

Under the Weather

The saying "under the weather" is sometimes used to describe when people do not feel well. Draw a picture to show what you think of when you hear the saying "under the weather." Write a description for the picture.

Fill in the Blanks

Read the sentences below.
Fill in the blanks with words from the word bank.

> germs   infection   prescription
>
> surgery   treatment   vaccine   virus

1. If you get a _____ from your doctor for a certain disease, you will not get that disease.

2. Some doctors are trained to perform _____ on patients in the hospital.

3. Listen to your doctor for the right kind of _____ that will make you better.

4. You may have caught a _____ from someone that made you sick.

5. If you wash your hands you will get rid of many _____ that could make you sick.

6. You may get an _____ if you do not wash your cut and keep it clean.

7. You will have to go to a pharmacy to fill that _____.

Here's to Your Health

Write a poem about your health. Use the words **germs**, **treatment**, and **virus** in your poem. Draw a picture to go with your poem.

Word Search

There are seven words hidden in the puzzle. Use the definitions below to help you find them. Then write the words next to their meanings.

```
B  T  R  E  A  T  M  E  N  T  F  V
I  N  F  E  C  T  I  O  N  R  I  A
C  T  S  U  R  G  E  R  Y  R  H  C
Y  E  M  L  E  G  N  I  U  B  C  C
Y  R  R  J  E  L  P  S  T  G  L  I
P  R  E  S  C  R  I  P  T  I  O  N
E  L  G  W  D  P  I  T  V  G  F  E
```

1. tiny organisms that can cause disease _____

2. illness or disease _____

3. medicine given by a doctor _____

4. medical care where the body is opened up _____

5. medical care _____

6. medicine that keeps a healthy body from getting a disease

_____

7. tiny organism that grows inside cells and makes us sick

_____

A Letter to Your Doctor

Write a letter to your doctor to thank him or her for treating you. Talk about the importance of health. Use as many of the health words you learned as possible.

_____

_____

_____

_____

_____

_____

_____

_____

Let's Go Over That Again

Review. Choose the correct answer to the questions below.

1. A kind of tiny organism that makes people sick is a
_____.

   a. virus
   b. surgery
   c. prescription

2. You should wash your hands often to get rid of
_____.

   a. surgery
   b. germs
   c. vaccine

3. A doctor can sometimes perform _____
to fix something inside the body.

   a. vaccine
   b. surgery
   c. prescription

4. A medicine that you get at a pharmacy is called a
_____.

   a. infection
   b. virus
   c. prescription

5. A medicine that keeps you from getting a disease in the first place is a
_____.

    a. germ
    b. vaccine
    c. virus

6. When a cut becomes red, puffy, or painful, you may have
_____.

    a. an infection
    b. a prescription
    c. a vaccine

7. A doctor will try to give you the best _____ to make you better.
    a. infection
    b. virus
    c. treatment

8. Write a sentence that uses the words **infection** and **prescription**.

_____

_____

Music All Around Me

Read the story. Then answer the questions below.

Maddie wants to be a composer and write the most beautiful symphony anyone has ever heard. She would make the tempo slow and the pitch low. She wasn't yet sure what the harmony would be like. Sometimes music will enter her head and she will sing it to herself until she can write it down.

Maddie always drummed different rhythms on her lap or on a table when they popped into her mind. She could use a table as a percussion instrument if she was away from her drum set. She wanted all of her friends to sing in unison, "Maddie loves music!"

1. From reading the passage, what do you think a **composer** is?

_____

2. What do you think the word **tempo** refers to?

   a. instruments   **b.** writing   **c.** speed

3. What kind of instrument do you think a **percussion** instrument is?

   a. one that you hit   **b.** one that you pluck   **c.** one that you blow into

4. What kind of **pitch** does Maddie want her song to have?

_____

Crossword Time!

Solve the crossword puzzle.

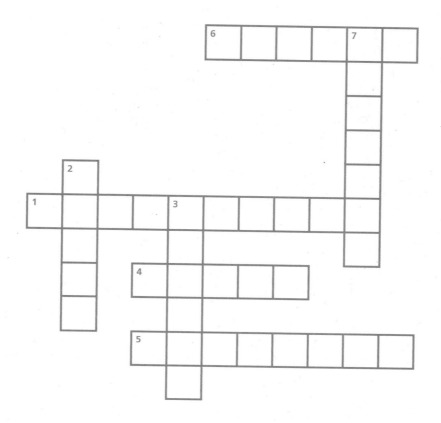

Across

1. a kind of instrument that makes sound when it is struck
4. how high or low a sound is
5. a person who writes music
6. a regular, repeating pattern of music

Down

2. the speed of a piece of music
3. all together
7. the combination of musical notes that make up a song

Fill in the Blanks

Use the words in the word box below to fill in the blanks.

composer   harmony   pitch   rhythm

tempo   unison   percussion

1. When people all sing at once, they sing in _____.

2. A drum is a kind of _____ instrument.

3. When you talk about how fast or slow music is, you talk about its
_____.

4. When you talk about how high or low a sound is, you are talking
about _____.

5. A regular, repeating pattern of music is called _____.

6. A person who writes music is called a _____.

7. The combination of single notes to make a song is called a
_____.

Your Favorite Music

Think about one of your favorite songs. Describe what its tempo and pitch are like. What kind of rhythm and harmony does it have?

_____

_____

_____

_____

_____

_____

_____

Percussion Discussion

A percussion instrument is hit or struck to make sound.
Think of things that you can strike to make a nice sound. Use the word
"percussion" below to begin each word. The first one is done for you.

PLASTIC BOTTLE _____

E _____

R _____

C _____

U _____

S _____

S _____

I _____

O _____

N _____

Your Favorite Instrument

What is your favorite musical instrument? Make a riddle about your instrument. Fill in the blanks about your favorite instrument. Then ask someone to try to guess the instrument.

1. My favorite instrument makes a _____ sound.

2. It makes a _____ pitch when you play it.

3. The instrument makes a sound when you _____.

4. It is heard a lot in bands that _____.

5. The song _____ uses my favorite instrument.

6. Here is a picture of my favorite instrument.

Did you guess it? My favorite instrument is a _____.

Let's Go Over That Again

Review. Write the meaning of each word below.

1. composer _____

_____

2. harmony _____

_____

3. pitch _____

_____

4. rhythm _____

_____

5. tempo _____

_____

6. unison _____

_____

7. percussion _____

_____

Review. Fill in the blanks.

8. A pitch can be _____ or _____.

9. Everyone in class sang the song in _____, or all together.

10. A drum or piano is a kind of _____ instrument.

11. I like songs that have a pretty _____ that I can sing to.

12. I can clap to a repeating _____ in a song.

13. A composer is a person who writes _____.

14. It is fun to dance to songs with a fast _____.

Answer Key

Page 4

```
J K I O M R W X J A
H F M E A S U R E P O X
F Q K I I O Z L L N
C W S V B N T T G N
A G R E E D E S T R O Y
T I R C R E S R J D Q S T
R M V E E S B R H U E
E E M V P B M N T Y A M
E E I B F A D R R A
C U N L K L Q F G E
E I U O W O R R A N
```

1. agree
2. destroy
3. enemy
4. flat
5. measure
6. narrow
7. stem
8. tire

Page 5
1. agree
2. destroy
3. flat
4. enemy
5. narrow

Page 6
stem; flat; tire; destroy; enemy; measure; narrow; agree

Page 7
Check students' stories for the correct use of the words in the box.

Page 8
Across
1. flat
3. measure
6. agree
7. enemy

Down
2. stem
4. destroy
5. tire
8. narrow

Page 9
1. long
2. heavy
3. hot
4. much
5. Answers will vary.

Pages 10–11
1. enemy
2. tire
3. agree
4. stem
5. measure
6. narrow
7. flat
8. destroy

Page 12
1. b
2. a
3. c
4. a

Page 13
Check that students' drawings and captions address the phrases "fight off her fears" or "rattle her nerves."

Page 14

```
G R E A G M X Y L W
C E N T U R Y J E T
A V S O I A K C B M
R F W C Y T P O D E
N O E T R L R T C T
I T H G I F E E Z C Y O
V E E B R T S Z E U S
A J D U Y M C H O P D
L S T R O N G E H
U M J D U Y M C H O P
```

1. attempt
2. carnival
3. cash
4. century
5. chop
6. fight
7. rattle
8. strong
9. toss

Page 15

Page 16
fight; century; strong; toss; attempt

Page 17
Across
1. carnival
2. rattle
3. attempt
6. chop

Down
1. century
4. strong
5. toss
7. cash
8. fight

Page 18
1. cash
2. chop
3. rattle
4. carnival
5. toss
6. attempt
7. strong

Page 19
Check that students drew something that was invented in the last century. Check that they wrote how the invention changed the way we live today.

Page 20
1. strong
2. toss
3. fight
4. attempt
5. carnival

Page 21
6. rattle
7. century
8. cash
9. chop

Page 22
1. b
2. c
3. a
4. b

Page 23

```
K G S O U U T W H E
B O U G H T B I J T V
I W O W F A I L D Z A I
C O M A F Q U U K G N T
N T E B R T C E F N I
V E F E V E R Y W H E R E
O U M G X O R K T O
E U N I T N O C O E
R S B V K L D Y D E
```

1. bought
2. continue
3. everywhere
4. fail
5. famous
6. negative
7. wild

Page 24
1. continued
2. bought
3. sell
4. fail
5. stopped
6. succeed
7. taught

Page 25
Across
1. bought
4. negative

Down
2. famous
3. continue
5. fail
6. wild
7. everywhere

Page 26
1. out of control
2. to go on
3. to do badly; to not succeed
4. law; less; ness
5. to make an area your own

Page 27
Check that students' word searches hide the words *bought*, *continue*, *everywhere*, *famous*, and *negative*. Check also that the sentences use the hidden words.

Page 28
1. succeed
2. unknown
3. sold
4. stop
5. positive
6. nowhere
7. calm
Sentences will vary.

Page 29
1. b
2. c
3. b
4. b
5. c

Page 30

Page 31

```
H S K R O W E R I F
Y R O S T O N E G X
R R B K L E O M T F Y
E L E V A T O R T Y R
B U I V K L A O T T R
E E T J Y R T L I T T E R
U L T B I C Y C L E P
L B E R H B S E U O
```

1. bicycle
2. blueberry
3. broom
4. doorway
5. elevator
6. fireworks
7. litter
8. stone

Page 32
Check that students underlined all eight words from the word box in the passage.

Page 33
Check that students' stories use all eight words from the word box and continue the story from page 32.

Page 34

1. blueberry
2. doorway
3. fireworks
4–6. Check that students use each word correctly in a sentence.

Page 35
Across
1. bicycle
2. broom
3. doorway
5. litter

Down
1. blueberry
4. elevator
6. stone
7. fireworks

Pages 36–37
1. b
2. a
3. c
4. a
5. c

6. a
7. b
8. a

Page 38

1. basic
2. foolish
3. forceful
4. outstanding
5. plentiful
6. special

Page 39

Students' pictures should show a baker with a lot of delicious baked goods around, and perhaps people tasting them and showing by their face that the baked goods are delicious. Students' sentences should describe drawing sufficiently.

Page 40

Check that the pictures students draw in the right column match the nouns and adjectives in the left column.

Page 41

Across
1. outstanding
5. forceful
6. plentiful

Down
2. special
3. basic
4. foolish

Page 42

1. basic (Check that students use the word correctly in a sentence.)
2. forceful (Check that students use the word correctly in a sentence.)
3. plentiful (Check that students use the word correctly in a sentence.)

Page 43

Students' descriptions should explain that you should not worry if you think a question is silly, or foolish. It is better to ask questions and be sure than to not ask at all.

Page 44

1. a
2. c
3. b
4. foolish, alone, social, basic

Page 45

Check that students' poems describe something or someone that is special to them.

Page 46

1. a
2. b
3. b
4. a
5. a
6. c

Page 47

special; outstanding; foolish; forceful; plentiful; basic

Page 48

1. correct
2. correct
3. incorrect
4. incorrect
5. correct
6. incorrect

Page 49

Check that student's drawings illustrate the sentences.

Page 50

1. dough
2. doe
3. mail
4. male
5. horse
6. hoarse
7. knight
8. night

Page 51

Across
1. flower
3. toe
5. see

Down
1. fair
2. wait
4. rose

Page 52

1. wait
2. night
3. rose
4. horse
5. cord
6. sale
7. flour

Page 53

Students should underline the words: road, hoarse, fare, hare, grate, rows, sail, flour, doe, hole
The corrected paragraph is: When I rode my horse to the fair, I was excited to see my friends. I could see that Jessica got her hair cut short. She looked great! She gave me a rose. She got it on sale at the flower stand near the front entrance of the fair. We went to get a snack. My favorite thing is the fried dough. I could eat a whole plate of it!

Page 54

1. great
2. grate
3. fair
4. fare
5. rode
6. road
7. whole
8. hole

Page 55

Sample sentences:
1. The boy plugged in the guitar cord so that he could play a chord.
2. The knight is out at night.
3. The people pay a fare to get into the fair.
4. The girl rode away on the road.

Pages 56–57

1. a
2. b
3. a
4. b
5. a
6. a
7. a
8. b
9. b
10. a

Page 58

1. autumn
2. harsh or unpleasant
3. right away
4. feeling bad for

Page 59

1. alive
2. autumn
3. bitter
4. capture
5. con
6. instant
7. magnify
8. pity

Page 60

Students should choose story 1 and make a drawing for it.

Page 61

Check that student's story uses the words *magnify*, *bitter*, and *pity*.

Page 62

Across
1. autumn
5. instant
6. pity

Down
2. bitter
3. magnify
4. con
7. alive
8. capture

Page 63

alive, autumn, biter, capture, con, instant, magnify, pity

Pages 64–65

1. c
2. a
3. a
4. b
5. c
6. a
7. b
8. a

Page 66

1. preview, prevent
2. dislike, disagree
3. midterm, midland

4. nonstop
5. into, indirect, inflate

Page 67

circle *take*, underline *mis*
circle *possible*, underline *im*
circle *port*, underline *ex*
circle *polite*, underline *im*
circle *safe*, underline, *un*
circle *heat*, underline *pre*
circle *cover*, underline *dis*
circle *side*, underline *in*

Page 68

1. review
2. nonsense
3. unhappy
4. telephone
5. forearm
6. inside

Page 69

1. preschool
2. dismiss
3. replay
4. undo
5. relive
6. uneven
7. repaint

Page 70

Across
1. unkind
3. review

Down
1. unsafe
2. disobey
4. relive

Page 71

1. preheat
2. unhappy
3. nonsense
4. disobey
5. unfair
6. redo
7. mistreat
8. uncover

Page 72

1. viewed before
2. un; not
3. obey; to not listen or not obey
4. possible

Page 73

1. before
2. not
3. not
4. again
5. not
6. not

Pages 74–75

1. pre; to view before
2. re; to paint again
3. un; not even
4. re; to play again
5. re; to live again
6. im; not possible
7. dis; to not obey
8. tele; system for sending sound
9. non; not making sense
10. im; not polite

Page 76

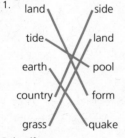

1. grassland
2. tidepool
3. landform
4. countryside
5. whirlpool
6. earthquake
7. landmass
8. mountaintop

Page 77

Across
1. mountaintop
3. whirlpool
4. grassland

Down
2. tidepool
5. landmass

Page 78
1. countryside
2. land and mass
3. bedroom and mountaintop
4. landform; a feature of the land

Page 79
Check that student's story uses the words *countryside*, *mountaintop*, *landmass*, and *landform*.

Page 80
Check that student's sentences start with the beginning letter provided, and check that they are about one of Earth's landforms.

Page 81

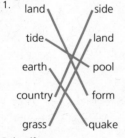

1.
land — pool
tide — land
earth — side
country — quake
grass — form

2. landform
   tidepool
   earthquake
   countryside
   grassland
   Check student's sentences for proper use of each word.

Page 82
1. grassland
2. landmass
3. earthquake
4. countryside
5. tidepool
6. whirlpool
7. mountaintop
8. landform

Page 83
1. earthquake
2. landmass
3. whirlpool
4. countryside
5. mountaintop
6. tidepool

7. landform
8. grassland

Pages 84–85
1. a
2. c
3. b
4. a
5. b
6. c
7. a
8. c

Page 86

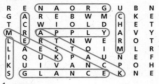

1. acre
2. apply
3. attack
4. charm
5. glance
6. groan
7. meek
8. skill

Page 87
1. b
2. c
3. b
4. a

Page 88
Across
1. apply
2. charm
4. skill
5. groan

Down
1. attack
3. meek
5. glance
6. acre

Page 89
Check that student's poem addresses the word *meek* and describes characteristics of an animal that children consider to be meek.

Page 90
1. apply
2. groan
3. skill
4. charm
5. attack
6. meek
7. glance
8. acre

Page 91
1. correct
2. correct
3. incorrect
4. incorrect
5. incorrect
6. correct

Pages 92–93
1. a
2. b
3. c
4. a
5. b
6. a
7. a
8. a

Page 94
1. citizen

2. country
3. history
4. liberty
5. picket
6. president
7. territory
8. vote

Page 95
1. United States
2. someone who is a legal member
3. the past
4. doing what you want
5. you disagree with something
6. to make a choice
7. land

Page 96

1. citizen
2. country
3. history
4. liberty
5. picket
6. president
7. territory
8. vote

Page 97
liberty, vote, citizens, country, history

Page 98
Across
1. liberty
3. territory
4. citizen
6. president

Down
2. picket
5. history
7. country
8. vote

Page 99
Check that student's drawing represents what liberty means to them, and that their caption describes what they drew.

Page 100
1. liberty
2. picket
3. territory
4. history
5. president
6. vote
7. citizen
8. country

Page 101
1. f
2. d
3. a
4. h
5. b
6. c
7. e
8. g

Page 102
cheer*ful*, friend*ly*, rest*ed*, hope*less*, car*ing*, wish*ful*, jump*ing*, great*est*, proper*ly*, most*ly*, glad*ly*, present*ly*, grate*ful*, fear*less*

Page 103
1. est

2. er
3. er
4. est
5. est
6. er
7. est

Page 104
Check that student's sentences use each key word correctly.
1. er
2. er
3. or
4. or
5. or
6. er
7. er
8. or
9. or
10. er

Page 105
1. ian; one who works at a library
2. er; one who writes
3. ist; one who works in the field of geology
4. ist; one who works in science
5. ier; one who carries mail
6. ist; one who works on teeth
7. on; one who does surgery
8. or; one who governs
9. er; one who welds
10. ian; one who works with people's diets
11. ian; one who works with music
12. or; one who acts

Page 106
1. ful
2. ly
3. ly
4. ful
5. ly
6. ly

Page 107
1. less
2. ness
3. less
4. ness
5. ness
6. less
7. less

Page 108
adventurous, careful, foolish, happily, excitedly, fearless, dedicated

Page 109
1. friendly
2. fearful
3. teacher
4. greatest

Possible answers:
5. perfectly
6. wonderful
7. useful
8. trying
9. niceness

Pages 110–111
1. b
2. c
3. a
4. b
5. b
6. a
7. b
8. c
9. b
10. b

190

Page 112

1. humid
2. hurricane
3. tornado
4. atmosphere
5. blizzard
6. smog
7. thunder

Page 113

1. a
2. c
3. air that has a lot of water vapor
4. tornadoes and hurricanes

Page 114

Across
1. atmosphere
4. humid
5. tornado

Down
2. thunder
3. smog
6. hurricane
7. blizzard

Page 115

1. smog
2. tornado
3. blizzard
4. humid
5. hurricane
6. atmosphere
7. thunder

Page 116

1. atmosphere
2. blizzard
3. tornado
4. hurricane
5. smog
6. humid
7. thunder

Page 117

Check that student's story describes a weather experience that they have had.

Pages 118–119

1. A tornado is a swirling, funnel-shaped cloud. A hurricane is a storm with strong winds that may form over the ocean.
2. layers of gases surrounding Earth
3. smog
4. blizzard
5. humid
6. b
7. c
8. a
9. a
10. c

Page 120

adjective
adverb
article
noun
paragraph
preposition
pronoun
verb

Page 121

1. adjective
2. adverb
3. article
4. noun
5. paragraph
6. preposition
7. pronoun
8. verb

Page 122

Across
1. preposition
4. article
5. adjective

Down
2. pronoun
3. paragraph
6. verb
7. noun
8. adverb

Page 123

1. noun
2. adverb
3. verb
4. adjective
5. preposition
6. pronoun
7. article

Page 124

1. swim
2. new
3. the
4. Swimmers
5. around
6. patiently
7. We

Page 125

Check that children have listed words in each group correctly and written a paragraph in the last box.

Pages 126–127

1. a
2. c
3. b
4. b
5. b
6. noun
7. pronoun
8. verb
9. adjective
10. adverb
11. article
12. preposition

BONUS: Check student's sentences.

Page 128

1. treat
2. bear
3. scale
4. season
5. loaf
6. hamper
7. hatch
8. hails

Page 129

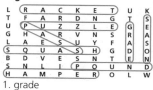

1. grade
2. hamper
3. pass
4. pound
5. puzzle
6. racket
7. season
8. squash

Page 130

1. pound
2. to be lazy, and a baked bread
3. a vegetable, and to mash or crush
4. a set of stairs, to go down to a level below

Page 131

Check that student's sentences use another meaning for the underlined word.

Page 132

Check that student's poems use the words from the word box.

Page 133

Check that students' drawings illustrate the sentence.

Pages 134–135

1. a
2. a
3. b
4. b
5. c
6. b
7. a
8. a

Page 136

1. baseball
2. doghouse
3. sidewalk
4. cupcake
5. snowstorm
6. butterfly
7. blueberry
8. downstairs

Page 137

1. horseshoe; a shoe for a horse
2. rattlesnake; a snake that rattles
3. hairbrush; a brush for a person's hair
4. mailbox; a box for mail
5. cheeseburger; a hamburger with cheese
6. popcorn; corn kernels that pop
7. raincoat; a coat for the rain

Page 138

1. foot
2. side
3. ball
4. boy
5. bee
6. lady
7. flag
8. ship

Page 139

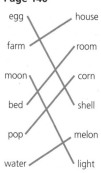

1. arrowhead
2. goldfish
3. treetop
4. seaweed
5. bedroom
6. scarecrow

Page 140

egg — room
farm — shell
moon — house
bed — melon
pop — corn
water — light

meat — ball
rain — bow

Page 141

Answers will vary, but may include:
1. campground, campfire
2. scarecrow
3. cupcake
4. bathtub
5. fireball, fireplace, firepit, firefighter
6. volleyball
7. junkyard
8. goldfish

Page 142

1. 9 total, 8 different
2. goldfish, farmhouse, sunrise, bedroom, underwater, afternoon, goodbye, backyard

Page 143

Check that students create and illustrate a compound word based on two of the smaller words from the word box.

Pages 144–145

1. a shell of an egg
2. a room for a bed
3. the sun that shines
4. a house for a dog
5. a storm of snow
6. shoelace
7. strawberry
8. cardboard
9. flagpole
10. starlight
11. spaceship
12. broomstick

Page 146

1. raining cats and dogs
2. time is a thief
3. shiny as an apple
4. in a world of hurt
5. all the world is a stage
6. working like a dog

Page 147

Check that student's drawings

illustrate the sentence "I'm as busy as a bee."

Page 148
1. the kitten is very cute
2. foxes are known as being very tricky animals
3. eyes that melt my heart
4. My mom thinks that if Nibbles does not learn to behave she could get into a lot of trouble

Page 149
Check that student's drawing illustrate one of the sayings from the passage on page 148.

Page 150
1. happy—"as a clown"
2. flat—as a pancake"
3. dry—"as a bone"
4. sharp—"as nails"
5. hungry—"as a wolf"
6. slow—"as a turtle"
7. cool—"as a cucumber"

Page 151
Check that student's writing includes at least three expressions.

Pages 152–153
1. b
2. a
3. a
4. b
5. a
6. a
7. b
8. c
9. c
10. a

Page 154
1. browser
2. database
3. download
4. gigabyte
5. hardware
6. memory
7. network
8. peripheral
9. software

Page 155

1. browser
2. peripheral
3. download
4. software
5. hardware
6. gigabyte
7. network
8. memory
9. database

Page 156
1. gigabyte
2. memory
3. browser
4. download
5. hardware
6. network
7. peripheral
8. database
9. software

Page 157
hardware, peripherals, browser, download, gigabytes, network

Page 158
Check that student's poems are about technology and that each line begins with the appropriate letter.

Page 159
Check that student's poems are about technology and that each line begins with the appropriate letter.

Pages 160–161
1. d
2. a
3. e
4. b
5. c
6. h
7. f
8. i
9. g

Page 162
1. generous—stingy
2. private—public
3. polite—rude
4. occupied—vacant
5. absent—present
6. minimum—maximum
7. narrow—broad

Page 163
1. deep
2. fresh
3. present
4. private
5. rough
6. rare

Page 164
Across
1. everyone
2. high

Down
2. hate
3. right
4. rough
5. sell

Page 165
Check that students' drawings illustrate the opposite of the word in the box.

Page 166
Check that student's sentences use the antonym of the word shown.

Page 167
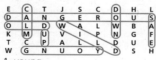
1. young
2. old
3. safe
4. dangerous
5. calm
6. wild
7. up
8. down

Page 168
hates, country, scarce, happy, calm, empty

Page 169
1. scarce, abundant
2. lost, found
3. below, above

4. sit, stand
5. hard, easy
6. great, horrible

Pages 170–171
1. b
2. a
3. c
4. b
5. b
6. buy
7. country
8. sit
9. inexpensive, or cheap
10. slow
11–14. Answers will vary but should be pairs of antonyms.

Page 172
1. germ
2. infection
3. prescription
4. surgery
5. treatment
6. vaccine
7. virus

Page 173
Check students' drawings.

Page 174
1. vaccine
2. surgery
3. treatment
4. virus
5. germs
6. infection
7. prescription

Page 175
Check that students' poems are about health and use the words *germs*, *treatment*, and *virus*.

Page 176
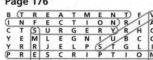
1. germs
2. infection
3. prescription
4. surgery
5. treatment
6. vaccine
7. virus

Page 177
Check that children write a letter to their doctor and use some of the health words they learned.

Pages 178–179
1. a
2. b
3. b
4. c
5. b
6. a
7. c
8. Sentences will vary.

Page 180
1. a person who writes music
2. c
3. a
4. low

Page 181
Across
1. percussion
4. pitch
5. composer
6. rhythm

Down
2. tempo
3. unison
7. harmony

Page 182
1. unison
2. percussion
3. tempo
4. pitch
5. rhythm
6. composer
7. harmony

Page 183
Check that students discuss tempo, pitch, rhythm, and harmony

Page 184
Check that each word starts with one of the letters in *percussion*.

Page 185
Answers will vary depending on the instrument chosen.

Pages 186–187
1. a person who writes music
2. a combination of single notes to make a song
3. how high or low a sound is
4. a regular, repeating pattern of music
5. how fast or slow a sound is
6. when music is sung or played all together
7. a kind of musical instrument that is hit or struck to make a sound
8. high, low
9. unison
10. percussion
11. harmony
12. rhythm
13. music
14. tempo